Cantinetta Antinori · Flavors of Tuscany

Allegra Antinori

Cantinetta Antinori

Flavors of Tuscany

Authentic Recipes and
Wine Recommendations

Photographs by Herbert Lehmann

Introduction by Carmen Wieser

CHRISTIAN BRANDSTÄTTER VERLAG

Special thanks to Caterina Aiuto, Nicola Damiani, Luca Chiesa,
Veronica Mazzoni, Paola Bettaccini, and Alessia Lana.

Photo credits:
Herbert Lehmann
Marchesi Antinori Archive, Florence
Alinari Archives, Florence

Bibliographic information published by the Deutsche Nationalbibliothek:
The Deutsche Nationalbibliothek lists this publication in the Deutsche
Nationalbibliographie; detailed bibliographic data are available on the Internet
at http://dnb.d-nb.de

First Edition 2011

Photography: Herbert Lehmann
Graphic design: fuhrer visuelle gestaltung, Stefan Fuhrer
Translation: Douglas Deitemyer
Print and binding: Grasl Druck & Neue Medien, Bad Vöslau

ISBN 978-3-85033-609-3

Christian Brandstätter Verlag
GmbH & Co KG
A-1080 Vienna, Wickenburggasse 26
Telephone (+43-1) 512 15 43-0
Fax (+43-1) 512 15 43-231
E-mail: info@cbv.at
www.cbv.at

Contents

Preface

The first Cantinetta was opened in 1957 in Florence's Palazzo Antinori, in the venerable tradition of aristocratic families offering products from their country estates for sale at their city palaces. Over time La Cantinetta Antinori evolved into a small restaurant. However, the fundamental idea of conveying Tuscan authenticity, tradition, and finesse through food, drink, and hospitality remained.

Due to the great success of the Cantinetta in Florence, additional locations were opened in other major European cities: in Zürich, in Vienna, and most recently in Moscow.

Most of the recipes in this book are taken right from the Cantinetta kitchen, and overall they represent an extensive cross-section of Tuscan cuisine, which has always emphasized simple, light, and tasty dishes made from fresh ingredients. Cooking according to the season is another Tuscan tradition: the foods we Tuscans enjoy eating most are the ones currently being harvested; these products are invariably the freshest, ripest, and tastiest. We also feel that the best way to appreciate good wine is to enjoy it along with good food, which is why we accompany nearly each recipe with a wine recommendation.

I wish you many pleasant hours enjoying the recipes and wines of Cantinetta Antinori in the company of family and friends!

Allegra Antinori

Cantinetta Antinori – Flavors of Tuscany

BY CARMEN WIESER

Celebrating the Tuscan lifestyle

Scarcely anyone who spends time in Tuscany can refrain from waxing lyrical about the beauty of this region: in summer the grain that glows like gold and the cypress trees that give the landscape its distinct character, or in autumn the fully ripe grapes that are transformed into a wonder of nature by the constantly changing play of color and light. One cannot help being touched by the splendor of Tuscany and delighted by its marvelous cuisine, delectable wines, and evocative atmosphere, for dining in Tuscany is like being part of a feast! Traditionally, a meal is celebrated with several courses: *antipasto* (an appetizer or hors d'oeuvre), *primo* (first main course), *secondo* (second main course), *contorno* (one or more side dishes), and *dolce* (dessert). Thus, a healthy appetite and sufficient time are absolute requisites for truly savoring the culinary specialties of Tuscany.

Cantinetta Antinori

Good food requires good wine, and good wine requires good food: in Tuscany food and wine represent an inseparable entity, and it is this very tradition that guides the famous Cantinetta Antinori. At the Antinori family residence, in a picturesque Renaissance palazzo in the heart of Florence, locals as well as visitors from all over the world can experience the "Flavors of Tuscany."

The side wall of the Palazzo Antinori still has a small window called a porticciola, *a reminder of the original idea of the Cantinetta Antinori.*

The idea behind Cantinetta Antinori goes back to an old tradition: in medieval times it was customary for Florence's aristocratic families to sell wine, bread, and other Tuscan delicacies from their country estates to the city folk through the small windows (*porticciole*) of their wine cellars (called *cantine*). One of these windows still exists on a side wall of the Palazzo Antinori. Today Cantinetta Antinori is a full-fledged restaurant, but with its authentic character and typically

Hunters with their kill; in the background the Passignano monastery, 1890

*"Tuscany represents the identity of Antinori,
and by this I mean tradition, culture, agriculture,
art, and literature."*

Marchese Piero Antinori

The symbol of the guild of vinattieri, or winemakers, at the entrance to Florence's Cantinetta Antinori refers to the admission of Giovanni di Piero to the guild in 1385, marking the beginning of the Antinori family's winemaking activities.

Tuscan elegance, it has retained the essence of this ancient tradition.

The first Cantinetta Antinori was opened in 1957 in Palazzo Antinori – one of the finest examples of mid-fifteenth-century Florentine architecture – in the ancient tradition of the *porticciola*. Directly behind the main gate of the palace is the entrance to Cantinetta, marked by the distinctive symbol of the guild of winemakers. In 1385 Giovanni di Piero became the first member of the Antinori family to be admitted to this guild. In the restaurant's strikingly simple interior one can still sample all the Antinori wines along with a selection of Tuscan specialties, many of which are prepared with ingredients from the family's various estates in Tuscany and Umbria.

Because this unique concept met with such success, Cantinetta Antinori restaurants were opened in other European cities: in Zürich, in Vienna, and most recently in Moscow.

Bread: a symbol of rootedness and simplicity

Down-to-earth and unpretentious but at the same time refined and culinarily exciting – this, in a nutshell, is Tuscan cuisine. This down-to-earth quality has its roots in the rural tradition of the region, while the simplicity can be attributed to the history of large sections of the country that long suffered from poverty: the difficult living conditions forced the people of that time to make do with cheap foodstuffs. What were once survival measures are now traditions: the unsalted bread (salt was very expensive in former times), for example, is still an important component of Tuscan cuisine. Whether as a simple side dish, as an *antipasto* in its typical form – as toasted slices of white bread topped with liver, cherry tomatoes and arugula, sausage, or *pecorino* – or as a *panzanella*, made of bread that has been soaked in water and then squeezed dry and mixed with vegetables: bread is an essential part of nearly every Tuscan meal.

Vegetables and herbs: only the freshest have their place on the table

The pleasing simplicity of Tuscan cuisine continues in the healthful side dishes, with their garden-fresh vegetables and herbs. The produce markets of Tuscany offer a rich assortment of seasonal products, which naturally vary according to the season. Thus in winter the people here fall back on various types of cabbage, legumes, artichokes, and mushrooms. A Tuscan would never buy tomatoes or peppers in winter or cabbage in summer! To these fresh ingredients are added only herbs of the season, which bring out the vegetables' own flavors. But herbs often play a leading role as well, for example as a side dish (*contorno*) in the form of deep-fried sage leaves and in main meat dishes like herb-crusted roast veal, rabbit with rosemary, or chicken in an anchovy-herb sauce. Fresh Mediterranean herbs such as rosemary, sage, and basil are also used together with the fruity olive oil of the region to lend certain dishes an elegant note. And olive oil has its own special significance, of course: it forms the basis of numerous Tuscan dishes, and the cuisine of this region would be unimaginable without it.

Meat and fish: no main course would be complete without them

Although Tuscan cooks take great delight in vegetables and make frequent use of them, the *secondo* course of an Italian meal unequivocally calls for meat or fish. Meat, in particular, plays a major role in modern Tuscan cuisine, from beef, pork, lamb, venison, and rabbit to poultry of all kinds. The Tuscans' particular fondness for grilled meat has a historical basis: in earlier times the open fireplace was often the only source of heat in farmhouses, and thus the fire was also used for cooking meat. This was done, of course, only on feast days, which is why even today, after the *antipasto* and before the *secondo*, the filling, carbohydrate-rich *primo piatto* (a pasta or rice dish) is served.

The meat course, as well, is enjoyed with plenty of bread and often a *contorno*, or side dish, of vegetables. When butchering, the frugal Tuscans always make use of the entire animal, which explains the large number of regional dishes featuring offal. One of the most popular is tripe (*trippa*), which in cities is sold from carts along with bread as a *pane di trippa* – a tripe sandwich. While meat dominates in Tuscany's hinterland, fish is more commonly served as the main

Ox-drawn cart on the road to Campalto, about 1935

"In Tuscany we love the things the earth provides during their natural season of ripening."

Allegra Antinori on Tuscan cuisine

course in the coastal regions. Favorites include sole and *baccalà* (salted and dried codfish).

"Tongues of fire" and other legumes: both delicious and filling

Farm gardens produce not only herbs and vegetables but also nutritious legumes such as beans and chickpeas. They are frequently used as side dishes and in robust soups, pasta dishes, and spreads – so frequently, in fact, that the Tuscans are known in the rest of Italy as *mangiafagioli*, or bean eaters. Tuscany can, indeed, boast a large number of very tasty bean varieties, such as the delicate blackeye cowpea, the tender *coco nano*, and the fat, purplish *borlotto lingua di fuoco* ("tongue of fire"). Traditionally legumes are not soaked overnight, but rather simmered slowly at a low temperature, without salt, in a *fiasco* (a bulbous wine bottle) or in a clay pot with a bit of olive oil, often in the warm ashes of an open fire. This is a particularly good method of bringing out the unique flavor of these beans.

The perfect end to a perfect meal: cheese or dolce?

To finish off a festive Tuscan meal the diner usually chooses between cheese and a sweet dessert – but you can have your cake and eat it too! Many people like to enjoy both, and you can also consume them in whichever order you like. Well-known and popular cheeses include *mozzarella di bufala* (buffalo mozzarella), pecorino, *scamorza*, and *stracchino*. *Scamorza* is a pulled cow's-milk cheese; like mozzarella, it comes from southern Italy and is often smoked. *Stracchino* is a soft, white, cow's-milk cheese that originated in Lombardy.

No less tasty are Tuscany's sweet chestnuts, which are found in a great many desserts. These nuts sometimes grow to the size of a fist and are very rich in carbohydrates, which is why chestnut flour used to be known as "peasant flour" and well into the postwar years was valued as a filling, essential part of the basic subsistence diet. Their intense, sweetly nutty aroma makes chestnuts a favorite food even today, either roasted over a fire, incorporated into pasta dishes, or used in cakes and tarts. Tuscan cuisine features a myriad of other tempting desserts, from apple cakes and strawberry tarts to rice custards and almond *biscotti*. So there is much more to Italian desserts than merely tiramisu and panna cotta.

Wine: for giving a dish the elegant final touch

Tuscan wine is not only a noble beverage that every epicure should experience but also a delicious means of enhancing many dishes. A wine's full flavor and aroma unfolds in many foods through the reduction process. Thus a good wine lends a slow-cooked beef dish like *Stracotto al Pèppoli* an especially elegant touch, and ground-meat or chicken specialties are often given a lovely note with a generous splash of Chianti or Vin Santo.

The traditional cuisine of Tuscany reveals just as much to the visitor about the culture, history, and people of the land as do the buildings, art treasures, and landscapes. It is simple and unpretentious, and these regional delicacies, paired with the area's famous wines, ensure an unforgettable Tuscan dining experience.

Marchesi Antinori: wine culture with a grand history

Tuscany not only touches and delights both the casual visitor and the epicure with its natural beauties and culinary pleasures; the region also has fascinating stories to tell about its remarkable art and culture. One of the most extraordinary of these stories is about the Antinori family. This clan of aristocrats and merchants has been making wine for more than 600 years, running one of the oldest family businesses in the entire world. All around the globe, the name Antinori is today a synonym for Tuscan wines: tradition, passion, and instinct have made Antinori one of the leading Italian producers of fine quality wines. The Antinori family's most important areas of cultivation are Tuscany and Umbria. Its world-renowned vineyards, including Chianti, Bolgheri, Montalcino, Montepulciano, and Orvieto, have a total area of nearly 3,500 acres. The history of Marchesi Antinori has especially close ties to that of the Chianti Classico. The Chianti region is the location of the Antinoris' most important wine estates, including Tignanello, Pèppoli, and Badia a

Villa Tignanello

> "*There at Antinori ... from a ripe Canaiolo,*
> *I press juice so pure that it spurts, foams,*
> *and glistens in the glass.*"

Francesco Redi, Renaissance poet, court physician,
and official wine advisor to Grand Duke Cosimo III dei Medici, in his
dithyrambic poem "Bacco in Toscana."

Senator Vincenzio Antinori (1792–1865) with family

"*Our roots play an important role in our company philosophy, but they have never held back our spirit of innovation.*"

Marchese Piero Antinori

Passignano – situated between cypresses, golden-yellow sunflowers, and gently rolling hills.

The entrepreneurial spirit of the current generation of Antinoris has its roots in an illustrious family history in the business world. It all began in Renaissance Florence: silk weaving, wool trading, and banking made the Antinori dynasty one of the richest and most powerful of that time, even rivaling that of their friends the Medicis.

In 1385 the family ancestor Giovanni di Piero Antinori joined the Florentine guild of winemakers. This date marked the beginning of the Antinori wine business, although the present firm was founded several centuries and countless generations later: today's Marchesi Antinori was formed in 1863 by Giovanni di Piero's descendents Piero and Lodovico Antinori, along with Gugliel-mo Guerrini. Full of energy and enthusiasm, they reorganized the family's winemaking operations and modernized the four wine estates, and the results met with approval in many countries of the world.

Antinori family tree going back to the year 1188: the first family ancestors in Florence can be found at the beginning of the thirteenth century. In Calenzano, a community in the province of Florence, the Antinoris were known as early as 1188.

Courage to experiment

At the beginning of the twentieth century Piero added to the family possessions by purchasing a number of small vineyards in the Chianti Classico region. In 1905, after a visit to France's Champagne region, Piero Antinori invited Lucien Charlemagne, a noted French enologist specializing in the production of champagne, to San Casciano to oversee the development of the company's first sparkling wine using the "metodo classico."

The famous composer Giacamo Puccini, a friend of the family, was so excited to hear of the sparkling-wine experiment that he wrote in a letter to Piero: "Dear Piero, I've been told that you have produced a very aristocratic Champagne." Less than twenty years later, in 1924, Piero's son Niccolò caused a scandal by adding Bordeaux grape varieties to his Chianti – a practice that was unusual, to say the least, in Tuscan wine production at that time. By 1928 Niccolò had created the first vintage Chianti, the Villa Antinori Chianti Classico. Shortly thereafter he also presented the company's first white wine, the Villa Antinori Bianco. Niccolò's son, Marchese Piero, continued this innovative tradition, experimenting, for example, with early harvesting of white grapes, temperature-controlled fermentation in stainless steel vats, and the use of different types of oak for barrique aging. His interest in non-traditional Tuscan grape varieties led him to produce such wines as Cabernet Sauvignon, Cabernet Franc, Merlot, Chardonnay, Sauvignon Blanc, Pinot Blanc, Gewürztraminer, and Traminer – and with great success. This was followed by years of expansion and the introduction of new wines that today have taken their place among the great classic vintages. But in everything he did, Piero had only one goal: producing wines of the highest quality. Thus it was due in part to his indefatigable commitment that more stringent quality specifications were introduced for Italian wines. With the revision of the DOCG (*Denominazione di Origine Controllata e Garantita*) classification, the Chianti was elevated to a new level of quality: not only was the prescribed proportion of white grape varieties reduced, but also – and even more important – the production yield and the yield per vine were restricted.

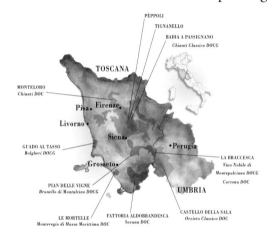

Tuscany and Umbria are the most important areas of cultivation for the Antinori winery. The family's vineyards cover nearly 3,500 acres and produce first-rate wines: regions such as Chianti Classico, Bolgheri, Montalcino, Montepulciano, and Orvieto have now become world famous.

Super Tuscans: the renaissance of the Chianti

The introduction in 1971 of the cult wine Tignanello represented a landmark in wine production. Together with the famed Italian enologist Giacomo Tachis, Piero developed a red wine from Sangiovese grapes, an ancient Tuscan variety, which he blended with Cabernet Sauvignon and Cabernet Franc to create a new type of cuvée, aged in barriques of French white oak. Freed from the restrictions of the quality norms for Chianti, which caused the wines to be slightly sour and often pallid, Antinori was able to create a completely new kind of Chianti, which can best be described as "elegant." This was a new beginning for the most Italian of wines, Chianti. Tignanello was hailed by international wine experts as one of the most significant wines in the history of Italian winemaking: essentially a simple wine, but elegantly aged. And this new concept deserved a new name: the term "Super Tuscan" was coined, and Piero Antinori was increasingly regarded as a worldwide ambassador of top-quality Italian wine.

The daughters take the reins

For twenty-five generations the Antinori family business has, without exception, been run by men. Now, in the twenty-sixth generation of the Florentine clan, three women are taking charge: Piero Antinori's daughters Albiera, Allegra, and Alessia. Today they control the fate of Europe's largest wine estate. The three wine experts are very consciously forging their own path, while – like the generations before them – always achieving a balance between tradition and innovation and following a family recipe that has proven itself for centuries: break gently with traditions to give new ideas a chance.

Piero Antinori and his daughters Albiera, Allegra, and Alessia. In the twenty-sixth generation of Antinoris these three young women now control the fate of this venerable business.

"The passion for wine, combined with the enjoyment of good food and hospitality, can be rediscovered at places full of tradition, such as Cantinetta Antinori."

Allegra Antinori on Cantinetta Antinori's recipe for success

Antipasti

Insalata di gamberi e carciofi

Artichoke salad with prawns

About 1 pound fresh prawns
3 very tender artichokes
3 tablespoons lemon juice
3 tablespoons olive oil
Salt and freshly ground black pepper

Blanch the prawns briefly in boiling water. Let cool, then peel. Clean the artichokes (removing the hard leaves) and slice thinly. Sprinkle them with salt and one tablespoon lemon juice and spread on a platter.

Arrange the prawns over the artichokes and allow them to marinate in the remaining lemon juice, olive oil, salt, and pepper. Makes 6 servings.

WINE RECOMMENDATION: *Bramito del Cervo Umbria IGT*

The artichoke has been cultivated in Tuscany since the second half of the fifteenth century. This tasty vegetable is prepared most frequently in winter and in the first months of the new year.

Bruschetta al pesto con pomodorini

Bruschetta with pesto and cherry tomatoes

12 sweet cherry tomatoes
Salt
1 teaspoon sugar
1 cup chopped herbs, consisting of:
4 parts arugula, 5 parts basil, 1 part mint
1 teaspoon pine nuts
¼ clove garlic
Pepper
¼ cup olive oil
8 slices country-style white bread

Finely dice the cherry tomatoes and place them in a strainer with a bit of salt and the sugar to release their juices.

In a food processor, finely chop the arugula, basil, and mint leaves. Pulse with the pine nuts, garlic, salt, a pinch of sugar, pepper, and olive oil to make a pesto. Fry (or toast) the bread, spread with the pesto, spoon 1 tablespoon diced tomatoes on top of each slice, and sprinkle with a little olive oil.

Makes 4 servings.

Crostini di zucchini
Crostini with zucchini

4 slices country-style white bread
One clove garlic, halved
2 zucchini
Olive oil
Salt
Vinegar

Fry or toast the bread on both sides, then rub one side with a halved garlic clove.
Slice the zucchini in thin strips, fry in a pan with a little olive oil, and arrange over the toast. Season with a pinch of salt, a bit of olive oil, and a few drops of vinegar. Makes 4 servings.

WINE RECOMMENDATION: *Scalabrone Bolgheri DOC Rosato*

Crostini con pomodorini e rughetta
Crostini with cherry tomatoes and arugula

12 cherry tomatoes
Salt
1 teaspoon sugar
1 bunch of arugula
5 tablespoons olive oil
6 slices country-style bread
1 clove garlic, halved
Salt and freshly ground pepper

Wash the cherry tomatoes, chop into small pieces, place in a strainer with a pinch of salt and the sugar to release their juices, and drain.
Clean and wash the arugula. Let dry and chop coarsely.
Sprinkle the drained tomatoes with 3 tablespoons olive oil.
Fry or toast the bread on both sides, then rub one side with a halved garlic clove and sprinkle with the remaining olive oil.
Top with the arugula, then with the tomatoes, season with salt and pepper, and serve. Makes 6 servings.

WINE RECOMMENDATION: *San Giovanni della Sala Orvieto Classico Superiore DOC*

Peperoni ripieni
Stuffed peppers

4 large green, yellow, orange, or red peppers
1 small red onion
1 large clove garlic
5 sprigs parsley
½ medium carrot, peeled and grated
3 tablespoons olive oil
About 1 pound ground pork
Salt and freshly ground black pepper
½ cup dry red wine
2 peeled tomatoes (canned)
1 slice prosciutto, pancetta, or cooked ham
(about 2 ounces)
1 egg yolk
2 tablespoon freshly grated Parmesan
¼ cup bread crumbs
½ cup vegetable or chicken broth

Soak the peppers in cold water for 10 minutes. Cut off the tops of the peppers, discarding the stems, and remove the seeds. Finely chop the pepper tops with the onion, garlic, and parsley. In a saucepan, heat 2 tablespoons olive oil and sauté the chopped ingredients along with the grated carrot 5 minutes until golden. Add the pork, season with salt and pepper, and brown 10 minutes. Add the wine and simmer until it has evaporated (6 to 8 minutes), then add the tomatoes and reduce the sauce until thick, stirring constantly (about 15 minutes). Remove from heat and let cool (20 to 25 minutes). Preheat oven to 375°F.

When the sauce has cooled, coarsely chop the ham and stir it into the sauce. Add the egg yolk and Parmesan and mix well. Halve the peppers and fill them with the stuffing mixture. Sprinkle with breadcrumbs and place in a large baking dish. Pour the broth and the remaining 1 tablespoon olive oil over the peppers. Cook in the oven until soft (about 40 minutes). Remove the dish from the oven and allow the peppers to cool for 10 minutes. Serve warm or cold. Makes 4 servings.

WINE RECOMMENDATION: *Vermentino Bolgheri DOC*

Scamorza ripiene
Stuffed scamorza

2 medium-sized eggplants
Salt
3 ripe tomatoes, seeded and diced
1 teaspoon sugar
6 small scamorza cheeses
(about 5 ounces each)
½ finely chopped onion
1 clove garlic, whole
3 tablespoons olive oil
¼ cup pine nuts
1 tablespoon pickled capers
1 tablespoon chopped basil
Peanut oil, for frying

Preheat oven to 350°F.

Cut eggplants into slices, salt, and let stand about 30 minutes. Place the diced tomatoes in a strainer with a bit of salt and the sugar to release their juices.

Remove the top end of each pear-shaped *scamorza* cheese and hollow out a cavity, leaving a ½-inch-thick shell. Cut the removed cheese into small cubes.

Rinse and pat dry the eggplants slices, then dice, fry, and spread on paper towels to drain.

In a large skillet, sauté the chopped onion in olive oil with the garlic until golden. Add the pine nuts, the capers, and the tomatoes, and cook over high heat 5 to 6 minutes.

Add the eggplant and continue to cook 2 to 3 minutes before adding the basil and the reserved cheese cubes. Remove the garlic clove.

Remove from heat and immediately fill the hollowed-out *scamorza* with the mixture. Bake about 5 minutes in an ovenproof dish.

Serve hot or warm. Makes 6 servings.

WINE RECOMMENDATION: *Scalabrone Bolgheri DOC Rosato*

Sformatini di spinaci in crosta di prosciutto

Spinach flans in a Parma ham crust

3 tablespoons butter
12 slices Parma ham
2¾ cups leaf spinach, blanched and drained
2 whole eggs
1 egg yolk
2 tablespoons milk
½ teaspoon nutmeg
Salt and freshly ground black pepper
1¾ cups ricotta cheese
3 tablespoons grated Parmesan

Preheat oven to 400°F.

Grease six small ovenproof dishes with 1 tablespoon butter and line with the ham slices. Squeeze all liquid from the spinach, coarsely chop, and sauté in the remaining butter. Whisk the eggs and the egg yolk with the milk, the nutmeg, and a bit of salt and pepper.

In a large bowl, mix the spinach with the ricotta and carefully fold in the egg mixture and the grated Parmesan. Fill the ham-lined dishes with this mixture and bake about 20 minutes. Unmold the flans onto plates and serve. Makes 6 servings.

WINE RECOMMENDATION: *Montenisa Franciacorta Satèn*

Cecina

Chickpea flatbread

3½ cups chickpea (garbanzo) flour
8½ cups water
¼ cup olive oil
Salt

Preheat oven to 350°F.

Blend the chickpea flour, water, and oil together in a large bowl. Cover and allow to rest for at least 1 hour, then skim off any excess water on the surface. Add salt, mix well, and pour into a greased springform pan to a height of at least 1 inch. Bake approximately 30 minutes in the preheated oven. Can be served with a few slices of *salame toscano*. Makes 1 flatbread.

Donzelle (Zonzelle)
Fried pastry

½ ounce dry yeast
About 2 cups lukewarm water
2½ cups flour
Salt
Peanut oil

Dissolve the yeast in the water, stir in the flour, add salt, and knead into a smooth ball of dough. Allow to rise at least 1 hour in a warm spot. Pour a generous amount of peanut oil into a pan, heat well, and fry the dough in walnut-sized scoops. Drain on paper towels, salt, and serve hot. (Goes well with sliced salami or a bit of *stracchino*.) Makes 4 servings.

WINE RECOMMENDATION: *Montenisa Franciacorta Brut*

Mozzarella in carrozza
Mozzarella "in a carriage"

8 ounces mozzarella cheese
12 slices white sandwich bread
4 large eggs
Salt
2 cups vegetable oil

Cut the mozzarella in 6 slices, then halve each slice lengthwise. Halve the bread slices lengthwise as well, and place each piece of mozzarella between two pieces of bread as though making a sandwich.
In a bowl, lightly beat the eggs with a pinch of salt.
Heat the oil in a frying pan to about 375°F. Dip each "sandwich" in the egg and fry on both sides until golden brown. Drain on paper towels.
Sprinkle with salt and serve hot. Makes 6 servings.

Crostini col cavolo nero
Crostini with black kale

1 bunch black kale (about 14 ounces)
6 slices country-style white bread
1 clove garlic, halved
6 tablespoons olive oil
Salt and freshly ground black pepper

Wash the kale, remove the tough ribs, and boil the leaves for about 10 minutes. Strain, reserving 1 cup of the cooking liquid.

Fry or toast the bread, rub one side with a halved garlic clove, and sprinkle with the cooking liquid. Shred the kale and arrange a few leaflets on each piece of bread.

Sprinkle with olive oil, salt, and a generous amount of pepper. Makes 6 servings.

WINE RECOMMENDATION: *Santa Cristina Le Maestrelle Toscana IGT*

Time seems to pass more slowly in the small towns and villages of Tuscany. It's well worth interrupting your stroll to enjoy a glass of wine and a deep breath of fresh air, especially when the first rays of sun warm the walls of the houses after a long winter.

Crostini toscani

Crostini Tuscan style

1 small white onion, finely chopped
1 tablespoon butter
1 pound chicken livers
Salt and freshly ground black pepper
¼ cup white wine
A bit of chicken broth
1 handful capers, chopped
12 small slices country-style bread

Heat the butter in a large saucepan and fry the chopped onion until golden brown. Add the chicken livers, salt, and pepper and continue frying 5 minutes. Add the white wine, cook until it has evaporated, then add a bit of broth.

Remove the chicken livers, dice as finely as possible, and return to the pan. Add the chopped capers and cook 3 more minutes. Spread each slice of bread with a bit of the mixture and, if desired, sprinkle with a bit of broth. Makes 4 servings.

WINE RECOMMENDATION: *Pèppoli Chianti Classico DOCG*

Crostini alla salsiccia e stracchino

Crostini with salsiccia *and* stracchino

3 skinned and finely chopped *salsicce*
(see Glossary)
7 ounces *stracchino* (see Glossary)
8 slices country-style white bread

Blend the chopped *salsicce* together with the *stracchino* to form a homogenous mixture.
Spread on the bread and bake several minutes in a hot oven. Makes 4 servings.

WINE RECOMMENDATION: *Sabazio La Braccesca Rosso di Montepulciano DOC*

Frittata di porri
Frittata of leeks

5 large leeks
4 tablespoons olive oil
Salt, freshly ground black pepper
6 eggs

Wash the leeks thoroughly, remove the green parts, and cut into ½-inch rings. Soak the leek rings in cold water for 30 minutes, then carefully rinse them under cold running water.

Heat 3 tablespoons of the olive oil in a flameproof casserole, season the leeks with salt and pepper, and sauté them until soft (about 30 minutes). Let cool.

In a large bowl, whisk the eggs with a bit of salt, add the cooled leeks, and mix well.

In a large omelet pan, heat the remaining 1 tablespoon olive oil over medium heat and add the egg-leek mixture to the pan. As soon as the eggs are set and the frittata detaches from the bottom of the pan, place a large plate, face down, over the pan, take a firm grip, and unmold the frittata onto the plate.

Place the pan on the stove again, and carefully slide the frittata in so the other side cooks. After 2 minutes, invert the frittata onto a plate again. Serve hot or cold. Makes 4 servings.

WINE RECOMMENDATION: *Santa Cristina Rosato Toscana IGT*

Terrina di faraona

Terrine of guinea fowl

1 skinned, boned guinea fowl
(about 2¼ pounds)
½ cup cognac
Thyme, chopped
4 poultry livers (from chicken or guinea
fowl)
Bay leaves
Sage, chopped
1 small finely chopped shallot
Olive oil
½ cup Vin Santo
Salt and freshly ground black pepper
7 ounces cooked ham
1 soft roll or 2 slices white sandwich bread
1 cup cream
1 egg, slightly beaten
1 teaspoon orange peel
2 heaping tablespoons pistachios, chopped

Preheat oven to 400°F. Cube the guinea fowl breast and marinate with the cognac and thyme. Thoroughly clean the livers and fry with the bay leaves, some of the sage, and the chopped shallot in a bit of oil. Deglaze with 2 or 3 tablespoons Vin Santo and season with salt and pepper.

Pass the guinea fowl meat (except the breast), the ham, and the poultry livers through a food mill. Dip the bread in half of the cream and squeeze out excess. Combine the meat mixture, the egg, the creamed bread, the orange peel, and the chopped pistachios. Season to taste with salt and pepper, and add the remaining cream, more chopped sage, chopped thyme, and Vin Santo as desired.

Line the bottom of a terrine form with several bay leaves and spread with half the mixture, then add the cubed guinea fowl breast (removed from the marinade) and top with the remaining meat mixture. Cook, in a covered bain-marie, in the preheated oven for about 1 hour 15 minutes, lowering the temperature to 350°F after 30 minutes.

Remove the terrine from the bain-marie and weight it with approximately 2 pounds (a bag of sugar, meat hammer, water bottle, or the like). Let cool, then chill, preferably overnight. Serve the cold terrine with salad, toast, and butter.

Makes 8 servings.

WINE RECOMMENDATION: *Pietrabianca Tormaresca Castel del Monte DOC Chardonnay*

Primi

Risotto agli asparagi

Asparagus risotto

1 pound 2 ounces green asparagus
2 small onions
4 tablespoons (½ stick) butter
3 cups risotto rice (e.g., Arborio), uncooked
4 cups vegetable broth, hot
Salt
1½ teaspoons chopped mint
1½ teaspoons chopped basil
¾ cup grated Parmesan
Freshly ground black pepper

Wash the asparagus and remove any light or woody bottoms. Remove and reserve the tips. Chop the stems into small cubes. Finely chop the onions and sauté them in 2 tablespoons of the butter, then add the cubed asparagus stems (do not allow to brown).

Add the rice and sauté for 3 to 4 minutes, then add the hot vegetable broth and salt. Cook for 15 minutes, stirring constantly.

In the meantime, blanch and drain the asparagus tips.

When the rice is tender (the mixture should be *all'onda*, with enough liquid remaining to still move in a wavelike motion), remove the pan from the stove and stir in the asparagus tips, the herbs, the remaining butter, and the grated Parmesan. Season with pepper and serve. Makes 6 servings.

WINE RECOMMENDATION: *Mezzobraccio Tenuta Monteloro Toscana IGT*

Risotto agli scampi freschi

Risotto with fresh shrimp and prawns

2 whole cloves garlic

1 finely chopped *peperoncino* (see Glossary)

Olive oil

7 ounces prawns, plus 4 cooked prawns,
to garnish

7 ounces large shrimp

½ cup brandy

½ cup cream

½ cup puréed tomatoes

1 teaspoon Worcestershire sauce

1 onion, finely chopped

2 cups risotto rice (e.g., Arborio), uncooked

½ cup white wine

1 tablespoon butter

Salt and freshly ground black pepper

In a large saucepan, sauté the whole garlic cloves with the finely chopped *peperoncino* in a bit of olive oil. Peel and chop the prawns and the shrimp (reserving the shells), add to the pan, fry for about a minute, then add the brandy. When the alcohol has cooked off, add the cream and then the puréed tomatoes with the Worcestershire sauce. Stir quickly to combine and cook several minutes.

Make a broth with the prawn and shrimp shells and water. Meanwhile, fry the onion in a saucepan until golden brown. Add the rice and simmer while gradually adding the white wine and the prawn broth. Stir constantly. Shortly before the end of the cooking time, stir in the prawn sauce and the butter. Season to taste with salt and pepper and garnish each serving with a cooked prawn. Makes 4 servings.

WINE RECOMMENDATION: *Mezzobraccio Tenuta Monteloro Toscana IGT*

Mezze maniche ai fiori di zucca e zafferano
Mezze maniche *with zucchini flowers and saffron*

1 pound *mezze maniche* (a short noodle
similar to rigatoni; see Glossary)
About 16 zucchini flowers
3 tablespoons butter
Olive oil
Salt
2 cups cream
1 teaspoon loosely packed saffron threads

Cook the *mezze maniche* in salted water until *al dente*. Wash the zucchini flowers, slice, and fry in a skillet with the butter, a splash of olive oil, and a pinch of salt. Add the cream and saffron, bring to the boiling point, add the *mezze maniche*, and mix well. Serve very hot. Makes 4 servings.

WINE RECOMMENDATION: *Cervaro della Sala Umbria IGT*

Gnudi
Ricotta-spinach dumplings

1¼ cup fresh ricotta cheese
1 cup cooked, drained, and finely chopped
leaf spinach
3 tablespoons grated Parmesan
2 eggs
Nutmeg
Flour as desired (maximum ½ cup)
Melted butter

Preheat oven to 400°F. Drain the ricotta well and place in a bowl. Add the thoroughly pressed spinach, half the Parmesan, the eggs, a bit of grated nutmeg, and a bit of flour, mix well and let rest at least 30 minutes. Bring salted water to the boiling point in a large pot. Using your hands or two spoons, form the ricotta mixture into small dumplings, dust with flour, and drop into the salted water. When the dumplings rise to the surface, remove them with a slotted spoon and layer them in an ovenproof dish. Top with a bit of melted butter, sprinkle with the remaining Parmesan, and cook in the preheated oven 10 to 15 minutes. Serve hot. Makes 4 servings.

Tortelli alle fave

Tortelli with bean filling

For the *tortelli*:
2½ cups all-purpose flour
3 eggs

For the filling:
1 thinly sliced onion
Olive oil
2¼ pounds freshly shelled beans
7 ounces young *pecorino* cheese (*pecorino fresco*), plus *pecorino* shavings, to garnish
1 tablespoon chopped parsley
Salt and freshly ground black pepper

Knead the flour and eggs to make a smooth, homogenous dough. Cover in plastic wrap and let rest 30 minutes in a cool place (not in the refrigerator).

In the meantime, heat a bit of olive oil in a nonstick pan and sauté the onion until golden brown. Add the beans and salt, cook for about 10 minutes, and remove from the heat. Let the mixture cool a bit and place it in a bowl when it is lukewarm. Cut the *pecorino* into small pieces (about the same size as the beans) and add to bowl. Season to taste with salt and pepper, add the parsley, and set aside.

Using a rolling pin or a pasta machine, roll the dough into very thin, broad strips. Use a dough cutter of the desired shape and size to cut out dough pieces. Place 1 teaspoon of the filling in the center of each and seal the edges well, enclosing the filling. Cook the *tortelli* several minutes in boiling salted water (they will rise to the surface when done), drain, and season with a splash of olive oil, pecorino shavings, and a pinch of pepper. Makes 4 servings.

WINE RECOMMENDATION: *Cipresseto Rosato Toscana IGT*

Crema fredda di zucchine alla menta
Cold zucchini cream with mint

2¼ pounds zucchini, peeled
2 small onions (preferably *Cipolla rossa di Tropea*), peeled
2 tablespoons olive oil
3 sprigs mint, chopped
1 bunch basil, chopped
Salt and freshly ground black pepper
Sugar
2 tablespoons lemon juice
1 cup cream

Cut the zucchini and the onion into coarse pieces, reserving a few strips of zucchini. Boil with the oil until just tender (the water should barely cover the vegetables). Using a hand blender, purée the vegetables with the cooking liquid, the chopped mint, and the chopped basil. Add salt, plenty of pepper, a pinch of sugar, and the lemon juice, then stir in the cream. Allow to cool and ladle into soup bowls. Garnish with a few raw zucchini strips and a sprig of mint. Makes 12 servings.

WINE RECOMMENDATION: *Capsula Viola Toscana IGTa*

Like the beautiful landscape, delicious wine, and culinary delights, carefully tended flowers in handmade terra-cotta pots are a hallmark of central Italy. The pots make popular souvenirs, bringing a bit of Tuscan flair to any garden.

Passato di zucca con i gamberi

Squash cream with prawns

1½ pounds yellow squash
3½ cups vegetable broth
Salt and freshly ground black pepper
1 pinch of sugar
4 tablespoons (½ stick) butter
¾ cup flour
2 tablespoons grated Parmesan

For the prawns:
14 ounces fresh prawns
3 tablespoons butter
1 clove garlic, chopped
Peperoncino (see Glossary) as desired,
chopped
1 teaspoon curry
3 tablespoons white wine
Chopped parsley, to garnish

Cut the squash in thin strips and cook in 2½ cups of the broth. Season to taste with salt and pepper, add a pinch of sugar, and purée. Prepare a béchamel sauce from the butter, flour, and the rest of the broth. Stir into the squash purée along with the Parmesan.

Peel the prawns, cut off the heads, set aside the peeled prawns, and brown the shells and heads with the butter, garlic, *peperoncino*, and curry. Add the white wine and continue cooking 5 more minutes. Force the shells and the heads through a cone-shaped sieve to make a concentrated sauce. Heat the sauce in the pan and use it to briefly cook the reserved prawns. Ladle the squash cream into deep plates or bowls, place a large spoonful of prawns and sauce in the middle, garnish with chopped parsley, and serve. Makes 6 servings.

WINE RECOMMENDATION: *Fichimori Salento IGT*

Gnocchi di peperoni
Pepper gnocchi *with asparagus*

4 medium yellow bell peppers
3 tablespoons olive oil
Salt and freshly ground black pepper
2 egg yolks
1¾ cups flour
4 tablespoons (½ stick) butter
1 pound asparagus, sliced into bite-sized
pieces
3 spring onions, chopped
1 cup grated Parmesan

Remove the seeds from the peppers and cut them into long, thin slices. Stirring steadily, sauté the pepper slices in a casserole with the olive oil, salt, and pepper until soft but not brown (about 15 minutes). Remove from heat and let cool for 5 minutes, then blend to a smooth paste in the food processor. Add the egg yolks (one at a time) and the flour. Bring 3 quarts water to the boiling point, dip a tablespoon into the water, fill it about half full with the *gnocchi* mixture, and carefully slide the *gnocchi* into the boiling water. Repeat until there are about 8 *gnocchi* in the pot. When the *gnocchi* rise to the surface, continue cooking for 2 minutes, then remove them from the water and place in a well-buttered dish with low sides. Repeat until all the *gnocchi* are cooked.

For the vegetables: Sauté the sliced asparagus and chopped onions in olive oil, stirring constantly, until the asparagus is crisp-tender. Arrange the vegetables on the *gnocchi*, sprinkle with Parmesan, and serve. Makes 4 servings.

WINE RECOMMENDATION: *Fichimori Salento IGT*

Spaghettini mediterranei
Spaghettini Mediterranean style

3 cups peeled and cubed tomatoes
Salt
1 teaspoon sugar
2 pounds 3 ounces fresh tuna (cubed)
6 sardines in oil
½ cup olive oil
2 cloves garlic, peeled
1 cup pitted black olives, halved
2 tablespoons capers
2 tablespoons fresh oregano, chopped
3 *peperoncini*, chopped (see Glossary)
2 pounds 10 ounces spaghettini
Parsley, to garnish

Toss the tomatoes with a bit of salt and the sugar to release their juices. Heat a very small amount of oil in a large nonstick pan and begin cooking the tuna and the sardines. In a second skillet, sauté the garlic (whole), the olives, the capers, the chopped oregano, and the chopped *peperoncini* in the rest of the oil over high heat. After about 10 minutes stir in the tuna and continue cooking several minutes until done. Cook the noodles *al dente* and serve each portion with sauce and a parsley garnish. Makes 12 servings.

WINE RECOMMENDATION: *Roero Arneis DOCG Prunotto*

The mild Tuscan light seems to make even the stone lions guarding the house portal gentler. No wonder that lovers of peace and quiet have found their paradise here for centuries.

Panzanella

Tuscan bread salad

5 cups day-old white bread (such as
Tuscan bread or *ciabatta*)
Balsamic vinegar
Olive oil
4 chopped basil leaves
1 thinly sliced onion
4 diced tomatoes
Salt and freshly ground black pepper

Moisten the bread with water, squeeze out the excess, and tear in pieces. Toss in a salad bowl with the vinegar, oil, basil, onion, and diced tomatoes. Season to taste with salt and pepper and serve. Makes 4 servings.

WINE RECOMMENDATION: *Villa Antinori Bianco Toscana IGT*

Whether roasted, topped with imaginative ingredients, or prepared as here in a panzanella, bread, especially the traditional unsalted white variety, is an essential part of every Tuscan meal.

Zuppa di ceci e cavolo nero

Chickpea soup with black kale

2¼ pounds cooked chickpeas (garbanzo
beans)
2 bunches black kale
2 cloves garlic, chopped
2 *peperoncini* (see Glossary)
8 tablespoons olive oil
2 small onions
1 bunch sage
2 sprigs rosemary
2 sprigs thyme
Salt and freshly ground black pepper

Drain the cooked chickpeas, reserving the cooking liquid.
Purée half of them and set the other half aside.

Cook the kale until crisp-tender, cut in strips, and sauté along
with the garlic and *peperoncini* (whole) in 4 tablespoons oil.
Finely chop the onions and the herbs and sauté them in a large
skillet in the remaining oil. Add both the puréed and whole
chickpeas, season to taste, and add the fried kale.

Add the cooking liquid from the chickpeas (and, if necessary,
some of the cooking liquid from the kale) until the desired
consistency is achieved. Makes 12 servings.

WINE RECOMMENDATION: *Pèppoli Chianti Classico DOCG*

Minestra di farro

Emmer wheat soup

1 onion
1 stick celery
1 carrot
Olive oil
3½ ounces cured ham, finely chopped
1 bunch rosemary
2 cups *borlotti* (cranberry) beans (see Glossary)
1¼ cup emmer wheat (see Glossary)
Salt and freshly ground black pepper

Finely chop the onion, celery, and carrot and sauté them in olive oil. Add the chopped ham. In another saucepan, sauté the rosemary well with a bit of olive oil, then remove the rosemary, reserving the oil.

Meanwhile, cook the *borlotti* beans in plenty of water (if possible, begin soaking one day in advance). When the beans are done, drain and purée ¾ of them. Mix the puréed beans into the vegetables and add water, stirring constantly, until the desired consistency is achieved. Season to taste with salt and pepper and cook for approximately 1 hour.

Cook the emmer wheat for about 45 seconds in salted water. Let cool, then drain. Add the emmer wheat to the soup along with the remaining whole *borlotti* beans.

Serve drizzled with a bit of cold olive oil. Makes 4 servings.

Wine recommendation: *Sabazio La Braccesca Rosso di Montepulciano DOC*

Tuscan country interiors create a cozy atmosphere, with the wooden ceiling beams contrasting attractively with the terra-cotta floors and the white chalk walls. And if it's cold outside, you can count on a crackling fire in the hearth.

Crespelle alla fiorentina

Florentine omelets

For the omelets:
4 eggs
½ cup milk
1 cup flour
Pinch of salt

For the filling:
1¼ cup ricotta cheese
1 cup cooked, drained, and chopped
leaf spinach
1 egg
½ cup grated Parmesan
Salt and freshly ground black pepper

For the sauce:
3 tablespoons butter
1 cup flour
4 cups milk
8 cups puréed tomatoes
Grated Parmesan

Preheat oven to 350°F.

Stir together eggs, milk, flour, and a pinch of salt to produce a thin batter. Let rest at least 30 minutes.

Mix together all the ingredients for the filling. Season with salt and pepper.

Lightly oil a 6- or 7-inch nonstick frying pan and set over high heat. Pour in a ladleful of batter and tilt to evenly coat the bottom of the pan. Turn the omelet when one side is golden brown. Repeat until all the batter has been used. When all the omelets are done, spread at least 2 tablespoons filling over each and either fold or roll. Place the omelets close together in a greased ovenproof dish. Make a béchamel sauce from the butter, flour, and milk, and then add the puréed tomatoes (sauce will be pink). Pour the sauce generously over the omelets, sprinkle with Parmesan, and bake in the preheated oven about 15 minutes. Serve hot. Makes 4 servings.

WINE RECOMMENDATION: *Santa Cristina Rosso Toscana IGT*

Fettuccine ai funghi porcini

Fettuccine with porcini mushrooms

1 pound 2 ounces fresh *porcini* mushrooms
1 shallot
1 clove garlic
5 tablespoons olive oil
2 sprigs of small-flowered *nipitella* (sometimes called calamint; thyme may be substituted)
½ cup cream
3 tablespoons grated Parmesan
Salt and freshly ground black pepper
1 pound 5 ounces fettuccine *all'uovo* (see Glossary)

Clean the mushrooms with a small sharp knife and a brush (avoid washing if possible). Separate and dice the stems, setting the caps aside.

Thinly slice the shallot and sauté it with the whole garlic clove in some of the olive oil. Add the *nipitella* mint and the diced mushroom stems, and cook over medium heat for about 10 minutes.

Slice the mushroom caps and sauté them in the remaining olive oil over high heat, then add them to the pan with the stems. Remove the garlic clove and the mint and add the cream, cheese, salt, and pepper.

Cook the pasta until *al dente*, drain, and toss briefly with the mushroom sauce. Serve very hot. Makes 6 servings.

WINE RECOMMENDATION: *Vino Nobile di Montepulciano DOCG La Braccesca*

Ribollita

Tuscan vegetable soup

2 carrots
½ stick celery
½ small head Savoy cabbage
2 small bunches Swiss chard (about 14 ounces)
1 bunch black kale (about 14 ounces)
1 onion
2 tablespoons coarsely chopped herbs (sage, rosemary, thyme, and basil)
10 tablespoons olive oil
2 tablespoons tomato paste
2½ cups *cannellini* beans (soaked overnight in cold water)
1 cup peeled, whole tomatoes
6 cups vegetable broth
Salt
½ loaf country-style bread, sliced
Freshly ground black pepper

Ribollita is a very thick soup, almost a stew. Wash the vegetables, cut them into small pieces, and finely chop the onion. In a large pot (preferably terra-cotta), sauté the onion and the herbs in half of the olive oil, then add the tomato paste, the vegetables (except the tomatoes), and the beans. Continue cooking for several minutes, stirring constantly. Then add the peeled tomatoes and the broth. Add salt to taste, cover, and cook 1½ hours.

In another pot, layer the soup and the slices of bread, then add 2 to 3 tablespoons olive oil.

Let stand several minutes and season to taste with olive oil and freshly ground pepper. Makes 6 servings.

WINE RECOMMENDATION: *Santa Cristina Rosso IGT*

Pasta e fagioli

Bean soup with noodles

2 cups *cannellini* beans
1 thin slice prosciutto rind
1 small potato
1 medium red onion, peeled
2 large cloves garlic, peeled
¼ cup olive oil
10 cups cold water
1 cup canned tomatoes, drained
9 ounces good Italian noodles (medium-sized conchiglie or lumaconi)
2 heaping tablespoons freshly grated Parmesan
Salt, freshly ground black pepper

Soak the beans overnight in cold water, then strain. Boil the prosciutto rind 2 minutes, then rinse with cold water and cut into small pieces. Peel and dice the potato. Coarsely chop the onion and the garlic and fry in olive oil in a soup pot over low heat until golden brown. Add the beans, the potato, the cold water, the tomatoes, and the pieces of prosciutto rind. Cover and cook about 45 minutes, or until the beans are tender but firm. Season to taste with salt and pepper, add the noodles, and cook 9 to 12 minutes, until the noodles are *al dente*. Let cool 10 minutes, sprinkle with the cheese and freshly ground pepper, and serve. Makes 6 servings.

WINE RECOMMENDATION: *Vie Cave Maremma Toscana IGT Fattoria Aldobrandesca*

Restaurants in Tuscany are often passed on from generation to generation. The lovingly crafted recipes also stay "in the family." You have to be a regular customer with a lot of persistence to find out just which herb lends a certain dish its savory character…

Zuppa di lenticchie, cavolo nero e zucca

Lentil, black kale, and squash soup

1 sprig of thyme

3 sage leaves

1 bay leaf

2 shallots or 1 medium-sized onion

1 carrot

1 tablespoon curry

A bit of chopped *peperoncino* (see Glossary)

8 tablespoons olive oil

2 cups lentils (preferably from Castelluccio; see Glossary)

6 ripe cherry tomatoes

Salt and freshly ground black pepper

1 bunch black kale (about 14 ounces)

1 piece yellow squash (about 14 ounces)

1 clove garlic

Sugar

Finely chop the herbs and shallots, and coarsely chop the carrot. In a pot (preferably terra-cotta, but any pot with high sides will do), sauté the herbs, bay leaf, shallots (onion), curry, *peperoncino*, and the carrot in about 5 tablespoons of the olive oil. Then add the lentils and the whole cherry tomatoes, season with salt and pepper, and continue cooking several minutes. Add hot water until the lentils are covered by about 1½ inches and continue cooking.

Cook the kale until crisp-tender, drain (reserving one cup of the cooking liquid) and shred coarsely.

Slice the squash and fry with the whole garlic clove in the remaining oil until tender but still firm. About 10 minutes before the lentils are done (after about 1 hour), add the kale and the squash. Season to taste with a bit of sugar, if desired. If the soup is too thick, simply thin with the reserved cooking liquid from the kale. Makes 6 servings.

WINE RECOMMENDATION: *Torcicoda Tormaresca Salento IGT*

Insalata tiepida di lenticchie

Warm lentil salad

1½ cups brown lentils (preferably the
Castelluccio variety; see Glossary)
1 carrot, finely chopped
½ stick celery, finely chopped
1 shallot, finely chopped
2 bay leaves
1 bulb fennel with greens

For the dressing:
½ teaspoon curry powder
1 tablespoon orange juice
1 teaspoon lemon juice
1 teaspoon balsamic vinegar
5 tablespoons olive oil
Salt and freshly ground black pepper

Cook the lentils together with the finely chopped carrot, celery, shallot, and the bay leaves in about 6 cups of water until the lentils are tender but firm. Drain.

Whisk together the ingredients for the dressing and add the lentils to marinate.

Quarter the fennel, then slice the quarters very thinly. Toss the lentils (warm but not hot) with the fennel slices, or simply spread them over the slices.

Finely chop the fennel greens (even better are fresh greens from wild fennel) and scatter generously over the salad. Makes 6 servings.

WINE RECOMMENDATION: *Achelo La Braccesca Cortona DOC Syrah*

Pasticcio di colombaccio
Wood-pigeon pâté

2 wood pigeons
8 tablespoons (1 stick) butter
1 carrot, finely chopped
1 stick celery, finely chopped
1 white onion, finely chopped
¾ cup white wine
1½ cups meat stock
2 egg yolks
2 egg whites
2 cups Vin Santo
Seasonal salad
Salt and freshly ground black pepper

Preheat oven to 320°F. Wash the pigeons thoroughly and pat dry. Remove and reserve the giblets. Bone the pigeons and fry the meat in some of the butter with the carrot, celery, and onion. Add the white wine and continue cooking, adding stock in small amounts, until the sauce is well reduced. Grind finely in a meat grinder.

Cook the giblets in butter, chop in the food processor, and mix into the ground meat with the egg yolks. Beat the egg whites and fold into the meat mixture.

Butter an ovenproof dish and fill it with the pigeon mixture. Cook in a bain-marie in the preheated oven for 40 minutes. Serve with seasonal salad and a Vin Santo reduction. Makes 4 servings.

Wine recommendation: *Il Bruciato Bolgheri DOC*

Rain, moisture, and cold winds lend the terra-cotta ornaments on the house walls their distinguished patina. Even the chubby faces of the cherubs seem mature and wise after being weathered by the winter storms.

Gnocchi di semolino

Baked semolina gnocchi

5 cups milk
8 tablespoons (1 stick) butter
Salt, freshly ground black pepper
Freshly grated nutmeg
1¼ cups very fine semolina (see Glossary)
4 egg yolks
1¾ cups freshly grated Parmesan

Set aside 2 tablespoons of milk and heat the remaining milk in a flameproof casserole. Just before it foams, add 4 tablespoons (½ stick) butter and a pinch each of salt, pepper, and nutmeg, then add the semolina slowly and steadily, stirring constantly. When all the semolina has been added, immediately turn up the heat so that the liquid reaches the boiling point as quickly as possible (prevents clumping). Then lower the heat and continue to cook the mixture 15 to 20 minutes, stirring constantly, until it is smooth and homogenous. Remove from heat and let cool 10 minutes.

Whisk the egg yolks with the reserved 2 tablespoons milk and add to the semolina mixture. Stir in half of the Parmesan and continue stirring to prevent the mixture from becoming gluey. Grease a marble or melamine surface and turn the semolina mixture onto it. Using a spatula moistened in warm water, spread the mixture to make a sheet about ½ inch thick, and allow to rest about 1½ hours.

In the meantime, melt the remaining butter in a saucepan and preheat the oven to 400°F.

Using a round cookie cutter (with a diameter of about 2 inches), cut slices from the semolina mixture and lay them in a buttered baking dish. Pour a bit of melted butter and some of the remaining cheese over the *gnocchi*. Make additional layers until all the dough has been used, finishing with semolina slices.

Place the baking dish in the preheated oven and bake until the surface is golden brown (25 to 30 minutes). Sprinkle with Parmesan and serve hot. Makes 4 servings.

WINE RECOMMENDATION: *Néprica Tormaresca Rosso Puglia IGT*

Secondi

Asparagi alla fiorentina

Asparagus Florentine

4 eggs
3 pounds green asparagus
Kitchen twine
Coarsely ground salt
12 tablespoons (1½ sticks or ¾ cup) butter
½ cup freshly grated Parmesan
Salt, freshly ground black pepper

Remove the eggs from the refrigerator at least one hour before using.

Wash the asparagus thoroughly and remove the light, woody bottoms. Tie the asparagus in a bundle with kitchen twine so the tips are even, then cut the ends so the spears are of uniform length.

Place asparagus bundle, tips upwards, in a large soup pot or an asparagus pot and add enough cold water to just cover the ends of the asparagus. Cover and bring to the boiling point. Add salt, reduce heat, cover, and continue cooking until the asparagus is nearly done (up to 20 minutes depending on the size of the asparagus).

Lay the cooked asparagus on a cutting board and remove the twine.

In a large frying pan, melt the butter and carefully fry the asparagus 6 to 7 minutes, turning occasionally. Sprinkle the grated Parmesan, salt, and pepper over the asparagus and continue cooking one minute until the asparagus is done, turning carefully.

Remove the asparagus from the pan (reserving butter) and arrange the spears on serving plates. Place the plates in a warm place.

Reheat the reserved asparagus butter. Separate an egg and carefully slide the egg white into the pan, reserving the yolk in its shell. Repeat with the other eggs, taking care not to let the egg whites run together.

Sprinkle the egg whites with salt and place one egg yolk on top of each, being careful not to break the yolks. Sprinkle each yolk with pepper, cover, and let simmer about 4 minutes.

Place the eggs next to the asparagus, sprinkle with freshly ground pepper, and serve immediately. Makes 4 servings.

WINE RECOMMENDATION: *Conte della Vipera Umbria IGT*

Zucchini ripieni
Stuffed zucchini

6 zucchini
1 small onion, finely chopped
5 tablespoons olive oil
1 egg
1 cup chopped bread, soaked in vegetable
broth and squeezed to release excess liquid
1 cup canned tuna fish (drained)
3 tablespoons grated Parmesan
1 tablespoon chopped parsley
Salt and freshly ground black pepper

Preheat oven to 400°F.

Wash the zucchini, cut off the ends, and halve lengthwise. Scoop out the pulp to make zucchini "boats." Reserve the pulp. Blanch the zucchini boats three minutes in boiling water and drain thoroughly.

Dice the zucchini pulp and sauté about 10 minutes in olive oil with the onion.

Whisk the egg. Add the soaked bread and the tuna to the onion-zucchini mixture and remove the pan from the heat. Stir in the Parmesan, the parsley, and the whisked egg, and season with salt and pepper.

Fill the zucchini boats with the stuffing and bake in the preheated oven about 30 minutes. Makes 6 servings.

WINE RECOMMENDATION: *Dolcetto d'Alba DOC Prunotto*

Sogliola alla livornese

Sole Livornese

4 small whole sole
Coarse salt
10 sprigs parsley
2 large cloves garlic
1 small stick celery
6 tablespoons olive oil
1 pound ripe tomatoes or drained, canned tomatoes
1 generous pinch dried *peperoncino* (see Glossary)
Salt and freshly ground pepper

Wash the sole thoroughly and rinse with salted water. Finely chop the parsley, garlic, and celery and sauté in 3 tablespoons olive oil in a frying pan about 10 minutes.

Pass the tomatoes through a food mill, using the disc with the smallest holes, and add them to the frying pan. Season to taste with salt and pepper and continue cooking 10 minutes, then remove the solid ingredients from the pan with a strainer-skimmer and set aside.

Add the remaining 3 tablespoons olive oil to the liquid in the pan. When it is hot, place all 4 whole sole in the pan, sprinkle with salt, freshly ground pepper, and dried *peperoncino*, and sauté 1 minute.

Sprinkle the sole with the reserved solid ingredients, cover, and cook about 16 minutes, turning the fish after about 8 minutes.

Serve very hot. Makes 4 servings.

WINE RECOMMENDATION: *Tormaresca Chardonnay Puglia IGT*

The red tile roofs and white stone walls of Tuscan country houses set off the deep green of the cypress trees. Anyone who has visited Tuscany will rave about the enchanting displays of color there.

Totani in zimino

Squid with spinach in tomato sauce

10 cloves garlic, finely chopped
2 red *peperoncini*, finely chopped (see Glossary)
1 cup olive oil
1 pound squid (such as arrow squid)
¼ cup vinegar
1 cup white wine
1 tablespoon tomato paste
1 cup puréed tomatoes
1 cup vegetable broth
1 cup cooked leaf spinach
Salt and freshly ground black pepper

In a large skillet, sauté 8 of the chopped garlic cloves and the *peperoncini* in hot oil until golden brown.

Clean and wash squid, cut into rings, and boil for 10 minutes in water mixed with the vinegar. (Don't throw away cooking water.) Remove from water and add to the garlic-*peperoncini* mixture.

Add the white wine to the mixture in the skillet, continue cooking, and reduce for about 10 minutes. Pour in the cooking water from the squid and reduce again (about 45 minutes).

Add a bit of water, the tomato paste, puréed tomatoes, and vegetable broth, and continue cooking for another 15 minutes.

In the meantime, chop the spinach and toss in a pan with hot oil, the remaining 2 chopped garlic cloves, salt, and pepper. When the squid is tender, arrange everything attractively on a platter and serve. Makes 4 servings.

WINE RECOMMENDATION: *Cervaro della Sala Umbria IGT*

Baccalà alla livornese

Livorno-style salted cod

4½ pounds dried, salted cod
1 cup flour
Olive oil
1 medium onion, finely chopped
2 cloves garlic, finely chopped
3½ pounds tomatoes, seeded and skinned
Salt and freshly ground black pepper
1 bouquet basil or parsley, finely chopped

Soak the cod overnight in water, cut into 2-by-1½-inch pieces, dredge in flour, and fry on both sides for several minutes in hot olive oil. Remove and drain on paper towels.

In the meantime, sauté the finely chopped onion and garlic. When the onion is golden brown, add the tomatoes and season with salt and pepper to taste. Boil down the sauce a bit, add the cod, and simmer for about 15 minutes. Just before serving, stir in the finely chopped basil or parsley.

Makes 6 to 8 servings.

WINE RECOMMENDATION: *Bramito del Cervo Umbria IGT*

Even on the hottest summer day, the stone-walled pools and fountains in Tuscan gardens provide a whisper of coolness as well as ensuring that the lush green plants and splendid flowers are able to survive extended dry spells.

Galletto al Chianti

Chicken in Chianti

1 chicken, about 3½ pounds, cut into 6 or more pieces
Salt and freshly ground black pepper
3 tablespoons olive oil
4 large cloves garlic, thinly sliced
2 tablespoons fresh rosemary, chopped
2 tablespoons fresh sage, chopped
2 cups dry red wine
¼ cup red-wine vinegar
1 tablespoon all-purpose flour
Chopped fresh parsley

Rinse chicken, dry thoroughly with paper towels, and season with salt and pepper. Heat the olive oil in a wide, deep pan and brown the chicken, a few pieces at a time, on all sides. Remove chicken from pan and set aside. Pour off all but 1 tablespoon of the drippings, stir in the garlic, rosemary, and sage, and sauté about 3 minutes. Deglaze with the wine and vinegar and return the chicken to the pan. Reduce heat to medium-low, partially cover, and simmer until the chicken is tender and the meat at the bone is no longer pink (about 30 minutes; slice into the meat to check). Remove the chicken from the pan and keep warm.

In a small bowl, whisk about ¼ cup of the cooking liquid together with the flour, salt, and pepper until smooth, then whisk into liquid in pan. Continue cooking over medium-high heat until the sauce is slightly thickened (about 5 to 10 minutes). Return chicken to pan and reheat. Before serving, spoon sauce over the top and sprinkle with a bit of parsley. Makes 6 servings.

WINE RECOMMENDATION: *Badia a Passignano Chianti Classico DOCG Riserva*

Coniglio al profumo di rosmarino
Rabbit with rosemary

1 onion, chopped

2 bouquets rosemary

4 tablespoons (½ stick) butter

½ cup olive oil

4½ pounds rabbit, cut into medium-sized pieces

2 cloves garlic, whole

Salt and freshly ground black pepper

2 tablespoons tomato paste

¾ cup wine (Santa Cristina)

In a wide, flameproof casserole, sauté the onion and the two rosemary bouquets in the oil and butter, then add the pieces of rabbit and the whole garlic cloves. Carefully brown the rabbit meat and add salt, pepper, and tomato paste. When the meat has taken on a good color, deglaze with the wine and cook over very low heat. If too much liquid evaporates, add a bit of water (not too much, or the sauce will be too thin). Makes 6 to 8 servings.

WINE RECOMMENDATION: *Pinot Nero Umbria IGT Castello della Sala*

If you travel through Tuscany in the spring, you will find the gently rolling hills and fields covered with a carpet of delicate blossoms. During this season the young herbs and vegetables fill the kitchens of the region with their fresh fragrances.

Involtini di vitello ai carciofi
Veal rolls with artichokes

3 tender artichokes
12 thin veal slices
4 tablespoons shaved Parmesan
12 toothpicks
2 tablespoons flour
4 tablespoons (½ stick) butter
2 finely chopped small onions
1 cup white wine
Salt and freshly ground black pepper
1 tablespoon chopped parsley
1 tablespoon chopped basil

Trim the artichokes (removing the tough outer leaves) and cut into quarters. Place a piece of artichoke on each slice of veal and sprinkle with a bit of the Parmesan. Roll up each piece of veal, secure with toothpicks, and dust with a bit of flour. Heat the butter in a pan, add the *involtini* and the onions, and sauté until meat is golden brown.

Pour in the wine, reduce for 3 minutes, adjust with salt and pepper, cover, and simmer over medium-high heat for about 30 minutes (adding a bit of water if necessary). Near the end of the cooking time add the basil and parsley.

Arrange the *involtini* on a platter with its sauce and serve. Makes 6 servings.

WINE RECOMMENDATION: *Bramasole Cortona DOC Syrah*

Agnello in fricassea

Fricassée of lamb

1 pound 12 ounces boned lamb shoulder,
cut into large cubes
1 finely chopped shallot
1 clove garlic
4 tablespoons olive oil
½ cup white wine
1 cup vegetable broth
2 egg yolks
1 cup light cream
1 tablespoon chopped parsley
1 tablespoon chopped mint
3 tablespoons lemon juice
Salt and freshly ground black pepper

Sauté the lamb meat and shallot in olive oil along with the garlic clove (whole) until golden brown.

Pour in the white wine and reduce for several minutes. Add the broth, cover, and braise over low heat until the meat is very tender (about 1 hour).

In a bowl whisk the egg yolks together with the cream, herbs, lemon juice, salt, and pepper. Add to the meat and stir for about 2 minutes. Remove from heat and serve hot.

Fresh peas are a good accompaniment to this dish.

Makes 6 servings.

WINE RECOMMENDATION: *Bocca di Lupo Tormaresca Castel del Monte DOC*

Insalata di pesce con fagioli sgranati
Prawn salad with fresh cannellini *beans*

1 pound fresh *cannellini* beans
2 cloves garlic
1 sprig rosemary
1 pound prawns, washed
⅓ cup plus 1 tablespoon olive oil
Juice of 1 lemon
Salt and freshly ground black pepper
1 bunch parsley, chopped

Cook the beans with the cloves of garlic (whole) and the sprig of rosemary in salted water until soft, then drain. Blanch the prawns for a few seconds so the meat separates easily from the shell.

Make a dressing with the oil, lemon juice, salt, and freshly ground black pepper, and marinate the beans and prawns in it. Sprinkle with parsley and serve warm. Makes 6 servings.

WINE RECOMMENDATION: *Cervaro della Sala Umbria IGT*

The Tuscan landscape is especially impressive shortly before a summer storm. The last sunbeams to permeate the towering clouds cast dramatic rays of light on the deep-green hills.

Baccalà in zimino

Codfish with green vegetables in tomato sauce

1 pound Swiss chard, chopped
1 pound firm, ripe tomatoes
1 teaspoon sugar
Salt
4½ pounds salted and dried
codfish (soaked)
2 large leeks, washed and thinly sliced
1 medium onion, peeled and thinly sliced
1 clove garlic
Peperoncino as desired (see Glossary)
3 tablespoons olive oil

Blanch the Swiss chard and drain well. Blanch, peel, and slice the tomatoes, then place them in a sieve with the sugar and salt to release their liquid. Cook the codfish for about 10 minutes, remove bones, and cut into pieces about 2 inches long. Sauté the leek, onion, garlic clove (whole), and, if desired, a bit of *peperoncino* in the olive oil. Add a bit of water and the chopped Swiss chard, cook for 5 more minutes, then add the codfish. Simmer for several minutes, add the tomatoes, and after 5 minutes remove from heat. Take out the garlic clove, arrange fish and vegetables on a platter, and serve very hot. Makes 12 servings.

WINE RECOMMENDATION: *Pietrabianca Tormaresca Castel del Monte DOC Chardonnay*

Carpaccio di pollo in salsa aromatica all'acciuga

Chicken carpaccio in anchovy and herb sauce

1 chicken breast (about 1 pound)
1 stick celery, coarsely chopped
½ leek, finely chopped
Juice of 1 lemon
3 bay leaves
⅓ cup plus 1 tablespoon white wine
2 cups water

For the sauce:
3 anchovy fillets
1 tablespoon capers, preserved in
salt (rinse with water)
1 teaspoon mustard
2 egg yolks
1 teaspoon lemon peel
1 handful parsley
4 or 5 celery leaves
6 tablespoons olive oil
Salt and freshly ground black pepper
Lemon zest, to garnish

Place the whole chicken breast with all other ingredients in a large saucepan (the liquid should just cover the meat). Bring to the boiling point; after 6 minutes turn off heat and let the chicken breast cool in the cooking liquid.

For the sauce, chop and blend all ingredients in a blender. Remove chicken breast from the liquid, slice thinly, and arrange on a platter with a generous amount of sauce and garnished with broad strips of lemon zest. Makes 6 servings.

WINE RECOMMENDATION: *Cervaro della Sala Umbria IGT*

Roastbeef al pesto di erbe aromatiche

Cold roast beef with herb sauce

2 cups chopped herbs, consisting of 6 parts
basil, 2 parts parsley, 1 part mint, and
1 part stick celery
¼ clove garlic
1 tablespoon pine nuts
1 teaspoon mustard
⅔ cup olive oil
1 tablespoon lemon juice
Salt and freshly ground black pepper
Pinch of sugar

12 thin slices cold roast beef
3 tablespoons shaved Parmesan

In a food processor, chop the herbs, garlic, and pine nuts. Add the mustard, oil, lemon juice, salt, pepper, and sugar, and mix well. Cover the slices of cold roast beef with the herb sauce and sprinkle generously with the shaved Parmesan. Makes 12 servings.

WINE RECOMMENDATION: *Santa Cristina Le Maestrelle Toscana IGT*

Some 5,500 olive trees grow on the Pèppoli estate, which lies about three miles northwest of Tignanello. Year for year the fruits of these trees are made into a vivid green oil with a particularly smooth flavor.

Terrina di carciofi alla parmigiana

Artichoke terrine with Parmesan

12 artichokes
Flour, for dusting
Olive oil, for frying
1 cup grated Parmesan
1¼ pounds mozzarella, sliced
Salt and freshly ground black pepper

Preheat oven to 325°F. Wash artichokes, removing any tough outer leaves, and cut into thin slices. Dust with flour and fry in hot oil until golden brown. Drain off excess oil.

Layer the artichokes alternately with the Parmesan and the mozzarella slices in single-serving flameproof dishes. Sprinkle with salt, pepper, and plenty of grated Parmesan, and gratinate for 5 to 6 minutes in the preheated oven. Makes 12 servings.

Pollo alla fiorentina

Chicken "alla Fiorentina"

1 chicken (about 4½ pounds)
Salt and freshly ground black pepper
4 tablespoons olive oil
4 small onions, sliced
1 tablespoon fresh rosemary, chopped
1 cup white wine
½ cup vegetable broth
½ teaspoon grated lemon zest
1 tablespoon rosemary needles

Cut the chicken into 8 pieces and rub with salt and pepper. Sauté the chicken pieces in the olive oil until the undersides are nicely browned, then turn and add the onions and the chopped rosemary. Continue to sauté for several minutes. Pour in the white wine, reduce for 3 minutes, add the vegetable broth, cover, reduce heat, and simmer for about 40 minutes. Before serving, season carefully with the grated lemon zest and garnish with rosemary needles. Makes 6 servings.

Flan di cavolo nero con salsa di cannellini

Kale flan with cannellini-*bean sauce*

1 cup *cannellini* beans for puréeing and
several whole beans for garnishing
Béchamel sauce (see below)
2 bunches of black kale
Olive oil
1 clove garlic, chopped
⅓ cup Parmesan
8 eggs, beaten
Salt and freshly ground black pepper
1 small onion, chopped
1 whole clove garlic
1 tablespoon chopped sage
1 tablespoon chopped rosemary
Diced tomatoes, for garnishing

Preheat oven to 400°F. Cook the beans until tender, saving a bit of the cooking water.

In the meantime, prepare the béchamel sauce: Melt 3 tablespoons butter over medium-low heat, add ⅓ cup flour, and stir until smooth. Gradually add 2 cups hot milk, whisking continuously. Add salt and cook for 7 to 8 minutes over low heat. Blanch the kale. Grease 12 small soufflé molds and line with a few kale leaves. Chop the remaining kale and mix with 3 tablespoons olive oil, the chopped garlic, béchamel sauce, Parmesan, and eggs. Season with salt and pepper to taste and pour the mixture into the molds. Cook in the preheated oven in a bain-marie for about 15 minutes. Sauté the chopped onion in olive oil with the garlic clove (whole), sage, and rosemary. Add the beans and simmer for several minutes, then remove the garlic and purée the beans, thinning them if necessary with a bit of the cooking water. Reverse the flans onto plates, pour several tablespoons of the puréed beans around them, and decorate with a few whole beans. Garnish with a splash of olive oil and 2 or 3 bits of diced tomato. Makes 12 servings.

WINE RECOMMENDATION: *Pian delle Vigne Brunello di Montalcino DOCG*

Anatra ripiena
Stuffed duck

1 finely chopped onion, divided

4 tablespoons (½ stick) butter

1 pound ground meat (veal and pork mixture)

4 ounces boiled ham, chopped

½ cup grated Parmesan

Salt and freshly ground black pepper

Nutmeg

3 egg yolks

3 tablespoons milk

1 duck (about 3 pounds)

½ pound caul fat

⅓ cup plus 1 tablespoon olive oil

1 sprig of rosemary, chopped

2 tablespoons tomato paste

¾ cup red wine (Tenute Marchese Antinori)

Meat broth

For the stuffing, sauté half of the chopped onion in a bit of the butter, then blend with the ground meat, boiled ham, Parmesan, salt, pepper, nutmeg, egg yolks, and milk to make a soft, compact mixture.

Bone the duck, fill with the stuffing, and wrap up firmly in the caul fat.

Sauté the remaining onion in a large skillet with the olive oil, butter, and rosemary. Add the duck and sear on all sides. Whisk the tomato paste together with the red wine and pour into skillet. Continue simmering, adding meat broth as necessary, until the duck is cooked through. Cut into moderately thick slices, garnish with a few braised shallots and fresh rosemary, if desired, and serve. Makes 6 to 8 servings.

WINE RECOMMENDATION: *Tignanello Toscana IGT*

Petto di tacchino ripieno
Stuffed turkey breast

½ boned turkey breast, about 3 pounds
1 egg
3 ounces skinned and diced *salsiccia* sausage
4 ounces ground veal
½ cup grated Parmesan
½ teaspoon coarsely crushed fennel seeds
Kitchen twine
2 tablespoons olive oil
2 cups white wine

Preheat oven to 350°F.

Rinse turkey breast, blot dry, lay on a cutting board with the skin side down, and cut enough meat from the thickest part to make ½ cup of finely diced turkey. In a large bowl, beat the egg slightly, add the diced *salsiccia* sausage, diced turkey, ground veal, Parmesan, and crushed fennel seeds, and mix well. Spread this mixture over the turkey breast. Starting with the short end, roll up the turkey and tie firmly with kitchen twine.

Heat oil in a deep, wide, ovenproof pan, and brown the turkey breast well on all sides, turning carefully. Pour wine over turkey, cover, and bake in the preheated oven for about 1½ hours, or until the meat is tender (the internal temperature should be about 180°F). Place the meat on a serving platter, cover loosely, and allow to stand for about 10 minutes. Meanwhile, skim the fat from the cooking liquid and reduce the liquid over high heat (you should end up with about 1 cup). Remove the kitchen twine, slice the meat, drizzle with the cooking liquid, and serve hot. Makes 8 servings.

WINE RECOMMENDATION: *Achelo La Braccesca Cortona DOC Syrah*

Arista in crosta di pane alle erbe

Pork loin in aromatic bread

4 medium-thick slices of country bread,
without crust
2 tablespoons mixed herbs (sage, rosemary,
thyme, parsley)
1 tablespoon freshly grated Parmesan
½ clove garlic, minced
Salt and freshly ground black pepper
5 tablespoons olive oil
2 egg yolks
1¼ pounds pork loin
½ cup water
1 tablespoon balsamic vinegar
3 tablespoons meat broth

Preheat oven to 350°F.

In a food processor, chop up the bread and mix with the herbs, Parmesan, garlic, salt, and pepper, then blend in 1 tablespoon olive oil and the egg yolks.

With your hands, firmly pat the bread mixture around the pork loin to make a coat. Place the meat in a large roasting pan along with the remaining olive oil, water, and balsamic vinegar. Bake for about 1½ hours in the preheated oven. Remove the meat and deglaze the pan with the meat broth.

Serve the meat sliced and covered with the sauce.

Makes 6 servings.

WINE RECOMMENDATION: *Guado al Tasso Bolgheri DOC Superiore*

A quick espresso in the morning, a small snack at noon, a glass of chilled white wine in the early evening – the bar is something of a sacred place for Italians: it's the place to meet, relax, and exchange news.

Spezzatino della cantinetta con patate

Cantinetta veal fricassée with potatoes

For the fricassée:
1¼ pounds veal, cut into large cubes
2 finely chopped onions
1½ teaspoons chopped sage
1½ teaspoons chopped rosemary
6 tablespoons olive oil
1 handful dried *porcini* mushrooms, soaked
in water and then squeezed out
1 tablespoon tomato paste
2 cups red wine
1 cup peeled and chopped tomatoes (fresh
or canned)
1 cup meat stock
1 tablespoon chopped basil
Salt and freshly ground black pepper

For the potatoes:
2 ounces pork lard
1 clove garlic
1½ teaspoons chopped thyme
1½ teaspoons chopped rosemary
1 tablespoon tomato paste
1 cup peeled and chopped tomatoes (fresh
or canned)
6 medium-sized potatoes, peeled and
quartered
Salt and freshly ground black pepper
1 cup vegetable broth

For the fricassée:
Heat olive oil in a large saucepan and sauté the cubed veal, onions, sage, and rosemary until the meat is brown. Add the *porcini* and the tomato paste, pour in the red wine, and reduce for about 4 minutes.
Add the peeled tomatoes, the stock, and the basil, salt and pepper to taste, cover, and simmer over low heat until the meat is tender (about 1½ hours).
For the potatoes:
In another saucepan, sauté the garlic clove (whole) and the herbs in the pork lard, then add the tomato paste, chopped tomatoes, and potatoes. Adjust with salt and pepper, add the broth, and simmer over medium-high heat for about 30 minutes.
Serve the fricassée hot with the potatoes. Makes 6 servings.

WINE RECOMMENDATION: *Santa Pia La Braccesca Vino Nobile di Montepulciano DOCG*

Arrosto di vitello in crosta croccante

Herb-crusted roast veal

4½ pounds veal silverside
6 thick slices of Tuscan bread, without crust
6 sage leaves
1 sprig rosemary
1 sprig thyme
1 handful parsley
2 tablespoons Parmesan
½ clove garlic, minced
Salt and freshly ground black pepper
6 tablespoons olive oil
2 egg yolks
4 tablespoons (½ stick) butter
⅓ cup water
⅓ cup white wine
1 tablespoon balsamic vinegar
¾ cup meat stock
1 handful dried mushrooms (optional)

Preheat oven to 325°F. Rub the meat with salt. In a food processor, chop the bread and mix with the herbs, Parmesan, garlic, salt, and pepper, then blend in 2 tablespoons of olive oil and the egg yolks.

Using your hands, firmly coat the veal on all sides with this mixture and place the meat, along with the remaining oil, butter, water, wine, and balsamic vinegar, in a large roasting pan. Roast for about 2 hours 15 minutes in the preheated oven. If necessary, augment the liquid with a bit of meat stock, and if desired, add a handful of dried, chopped mushrooms sautéed in a bit of butter. When the meat is done, transfer it to a serving platter, rapidly boil down the sauce, cut the veal into thin slices, and serve with the sauce.

Artichokes (sautéed in butter with a bit of garlic) are a fine accompaniment to this dish. Makes 8 servings.

WINE RECOMMENDATION: *Tignanello Toscana IGT*

Girello ai carciofi

Braised veal with artichokes

4½ pounds veal silverside
8 tablespoons (1 stick) butter
2 chopped shallots
6 anchovy fillets
3 cups white wine
8 artichokes
Salt and freshly ground black pepper
Lemon zest

In a large pot, heat the butter and sauté the meat until it takes on color. Add the shallots, anchovy fillets, and wine, cover, and reduce heat. Trim the artichokes, cut into slices, and after the meat has cooked for about an hour, add them to the pot. Simmer one more hour to ensure that the sauce is properly reduced. Adjust seasoning with salt and pepper. Slice the veal and serve with its own sauce and sprinkled with lemon zest. Suitable accompaniments are peas or mashed potatoes.
Makes 8 servings.

WINE RECOMMENDATION: *Vie Cave Maremma Toscana IGT*

Lemons bring freshness into the kitchen – and Tuscans know this: since the fifteenth century aristocrats have devoted themselves to the cultivation of a particularly robust variety that blooms from spring right into autumn. For this reason, one sees trees next to each other bearing lemons of widely varying degrees of ripeness.

Braciole fritte

Deep-fried veal or beef cutlets

4 boneless veal cutlets (about ¾ pound) or
thin slices of tender sirloin
2 large eggs
Salt
¾ cup fine unseasoned bread crumbs
2 cups vegetable oil, for frying (peanut oil
is a good choice)
Lemon wedges
Tomato, diced and sautéed (optional)

Dampen two sheets of wax paper, place the cutlets between them, and pound them with a meat hammer until about ⅛ inch thick.

In a large bowl, lightly beat the eggs with a pinch of salt. Lay the cutlets one by one into the beaten egg (they should be well coated with egg) and let them soak for 1 hour.

Spread the bread crumbs on a board and bread the cutlets on both sides, pressing the cutlets gently with your fingers so the crumbs stick to the bottom side as well.

Heat the oil in a frying pan. When it is hot (about 375°F), lay the cutlets in the pan one by one and fry about 1 minute on each side, until golden brown.

Drain briefly on paper towels, sprinkle with a bit of salt, garnish with the lemon wedges and, if desired, a few bits of diced, sautéed tomato, and serve immediately. Makes 4 servings.

WINE RECOMMENDATION: *Achelo La Braccesca Cortona DOC Syrah*

Stracotto al Pèppoli

Braised beef with Pèppoli wine sauce

2 slices bacon
1 clove garlic
1½ teaspoons sage leaves
1½ teaspoons rosemary needles
1¼ pounds beef for pot roast
Salt and freshly ground black pepper
Kitchen twine
¼ cup olive oil
2 coarsely chopped onions
1 stick celery, diced
3 carrots, diced
1 bay leaf
2 cups Pèppoli Chianti Classico DOCG
2 cups canned tomatoes
1 tablespoon chopped basil
½ cup vegetable broth

Mince together bacon, garlic, sage, and rosemary. Make small incisions in the meat and fill them with this mixture, rub with salt and pepper, and tie the meat tightly with kitchen twine for braising.

Heat the olive oil in a large saucepan or flameproof casserole, sauté the onions, celery, and carrots briefly, add the meat and the bay leaf, and sauté the meat quickly over high heat until golden brown. Pour in the wine and reduce for several minutes. Add the tomatoes and basil, pour in the broth, cover, and braise over low heat until the meat is tender (about 2 hours). Remove the meat from the pan or casserole and pass the sauce through a sieve. Slice the meat, pour the sauce over it, and serve. Makes 6 servings.

WINE RECOMMENDATION: *Pèppoli Chianti Classico DOCG*

Trippa
Tripe

2 finely chopped onions
1 cup olive oil
1 tablespoon tomato paste
2 cups peeled and chopped tomatoes
(fresh or canned)
Salt and freshly ground black pepper
1½ pounds cleaned and boiled tripe
¾ cup meat stock
3 tablespoons butter
½ cup grated Parmesan

In a stockpot, sauté the onions in a bit of olive oil, then add the tomato paste, the tomatoes, and a pinch of salt and pepper, and simmer for several minutes.

In the meantime, cut the tripe into thin strips, blanch, and then add to the stockpot and simmer for about an hour, continually adding small amounts of meat stock as necessary. When the tripe is done, stir in the butter and serve with grated Parmesan. Makes 12 servings.

WINE RECOMMENDATION: *Marchese Antinori Chianti Classico DOCG Riserva*

Just like the well-filled bread basket, wine is a fixture on the Tuscan table. There are many wines to choose from, and it is wise to trust the recommendation of your host – he knows the perfect accompaniment to every dish.

Polpettone alla chiantigiana
Chianti-style meatloaf

3 slices white bread, crust removed
½ cup plus 1 tablespoon dry red wine
2 pounds beef (top round or sirloin, in one piece)
4 sweet *salsiccia* sausages (*salsicce dolci*, without fennel seeds) or 12 ounces pork (in one piece)
2 medium-sized cloves garlic
4 large sage leaves (fresh or preserved in salt)
2 juniper berries
3 large eggs
2 tablespoons olive oil
Salt and freshly ground black pepper
½ pound thinly sliced prosciutto
Kitchen twine
½ cup all-purpose flour

For the sauce:
4 tablespoons olive oil
1 whole clove garlic
2 whole sage leaves (fresh or preserved in salt)
1 cup dry red wine

Stir the white bread and ½ cup of the red wine in a saucepan over medium-high heat until a paste has formed (about 5 minutes). Remove from heat and let cool (about 15 minutes). Cut the beef into 1-inch cubes and remove the skin from the sausages. Using a meat grinder, grind the beef, sausages, garlic, sage, and juniper berries all together into a bowl, using the disc with the smallest holes. Add eggs, olive oil, and remaining tablespoon of wine to the bowl and mix well. Add the bread paste, season with salt and pepper, and mix again. Arrange the prosciutto on a board with the slices overlapping to form an unbroken layer. Shape the prepared meat mixture into a thick cylinder about 11 inches long and 4 to 5 inches wide. Place the meat on the prosciutto and carefully wrap the prosciutto layer around it. Use a bit of thin kitchen twine to tie up the roll, then lightly flour it.

For the sauce: In a large skillet, heat the olive oil and sauté the garlic and sage leaves for a few minutes over medium heat. Add the *polpettone*, turn up the heat, and sauté on both sides until golden brown (about 1 minute each side). Meanwhile, preheat the oven to 375°F, transfer the polpettone to a large baking dish, pour the wine over the meat, and bake for 45 minutes, turning the meat twice and basting it from time to time with its own juices.

Remove the *polpettone* from the oven, transfer it to a serving platter, cover, and let stand for about 5 minutes. Then untie the meat and carefully cut it into slices approximately ½ inch thick. Makes 8 servings.

WINE RECOMMENDATION: *Marchese Antinori Chianti Classico DOCG Riserva*

Polenta con salsicce

Polenta with sausages

4 ounces dried *porcini* mushrooms
6 sweet *salsiccia* sausages, without fennel
seeds
1 finely chopped red onion
⅓ cup olive oil
¼ cup tomato paste
Salt and freshly ground black pepper
2 cups meat or vegetable broth

For the polenta:
2½ quarts water
Coarse-grained salt
1 pound coarse Italian yellow cornmeal

Soak the dried *porcini* mushrooms for 30 minutes in a bowl of lukewarm water. Meanwhile, halve the sausages, heat the oil in a large saucepan, and sauté the chopped onion until golden. Add the halved sausages and sauté lightly for 10 minutes, then add the tomato paste and simmer for 5 more minutes. Drain the mushrooms, add to sausage mixture, and season to taste with salt and pepper.

In a second saucepan, bring the broth to the boiling point, then pour it into the saucepan with the sausage. Simmer very slowly until most of the broth has evaporated (about 25 minutes).

While the sauce is reducing, make the polenta:

In a large pot, bring the salted water to the boiling point, then add the cornmeal, pouring it in very slowly while stirring constantly. When all of the cornmeal is in the pot, keep stirring until the polenta detaches from the bottom of the pot (about 20 minutes), then let rest over the heat for a few minutes. Arrange the sausages directly on the polenta and pour the sausage sauce over the top. Makes 6 servings.

WINE RECOMMENDATION: *Barolo Bussia DOCG Prunotto*

Contorni

Piselli al prosciutto

Sweet peas with prosciutto

2 ounces diced prosciutto
Olive oil
1 pound peas (freshly shelled, if possible)
Salt and freshly ground black pepper
A bit of chopped parsley
Several cloves garlic, whole
1 teaspoon sugar (optional)

Sauté the diced prosciutto in olive oil. Add the peas, salt, pepper, a generous pinch of parsley, and several whole garlic cloves (if the peas are not sweet enough, also add 1 teaspoon sugar).
Cook for 15 minutes, stirring constantly. Makes 4 servings.

Foglie di salvia fritte

Fried sage leaves

32 sage leaves (best harvested in May/June; the leaves are deep green and about two fingers wide)
2 cups all-purpose flour
2 eggs
Pinch of salt
8 anchovy fillets (in oil)
Olive oil

Wash the sage leaves and blot dry. Blend flour, eggs, and a bit of salt (not too much, as sage already has a slightly salty taste) to make a firm batter. Trim the anchovies, remove the bones, and cut into fingernail-sized pieces. Place a few anchovy pieces between 2 sage leaves (resembling a sandwich), dip in the batter, and fry in hot oil. Makes 4 servings.

Fiori fritti

Fried zucchini flowers

Male zucchini flowers (3 to 4 per person)
Flour as needed
Sparkling mineral water or beer
2 eggs
Salt
Olive oil, for frying
Vin Santo (optional)

Usually the male zucchini flowers are used because they have a long stem, unlike their female counterparts, which rest directly on the fruit.

Harvest the flowers immediately after they have opened, removing the stem, green leaves, inner pistils, and stamens.

With the flour, mineral water (or beer), eggs, and a bit of salt, make a smooth, creamy batter (it should just barely drip from a wooden spoon). Dip the flowers in the batter and deep fry in hot oil. If you prefer your fried flowers a bit crispier, add a splash of Vin Santo to the batter. Makes 4 servings.

The lower the sun sinks in the sky on summer evenings, the louder the chirping of the crickets becomes. And if you wait long enough – not a difficult task with a glass of good wine in your hand – you will witness a light show put on by the swarms of fireflies that are found here.

Carciofi ritti
Stuffed artichokes

4 large artichokes
Juice of 1 lemon

For the stuffing:
2 medium-sized cloves garlic
10 sprigs parsley
About ¼ pound pancetta or prosciutto, in
one piece
Salt, freshly ground pepper

For the second part of the dish:
1 small clove garlic, finely chopped
10 sprigs parsley, finely chopped
2 ounces finely chopped pancetta or
prosciutto
2 tablespoons olive oil
Salt, freshly ground pepper
2 cups vegetable or meat broth

Soak the artichokes for 30 minutes in a large bowl of cold water with the lemon juice. Then clean the artichokes (removing the tough outer leaves) and cut off the stems, saving them for the stuffing. Put the artichoke heads back in the water with the lemon juice and let them soak.

To make the stuffing, coarsely chop the 2 cloves of garlic and the parsley, and cut the pancetta (prosciutto) and the artichoke stems into small pieces. Place in a small bowl, add salt and pepper, and mix well.

Drain the artichokes, blot dry with paper towels, and stuff them with the mixture in the bowl, pulling the leaves apart and pressing the stuffing in between.

For the second part of the dish, mix the finely chopped garlic, parsley, and pancetta (prosciutto) together with the olive oil and spread over the bottom of a flameproof casserole (terracotta, if possible). Place the stuffed artichokes upright in the casserole and sauté over medium-high heat until lightly brown, about 5 minutes.

Pour half of the broth into the casserole, cover, simmer slowly for 15 to 20 minutes, then add the salt, pepper, and the remaining broth. Reduce the heat and simmer slowly for 20 minutes or longer (the artichokes should be tender but not fall apart).

Carefully place the artichokes on a serving dish, pour some juice from the casserole over each one, and serve either immediately (hot) or cold. Makes 4 servings.

Fagioli all'uccelletto

White beans with sage and tomatoes

¼ cup olive oil
6 large sage leaves, fresh or preserved in salt
4 large cloves garlic
1 pound very ripe fresh tomatoes (or canned)
Salt and freshly ground pepper
4 cups boiled and drained *cannellini* beans

Sauté the unpeeled, whole garlic cloves with the sage leaves in a flameproof casserole (terra-cotta, if possible) for 4 to 5 minutes in the olive oil. Pass the tomatoes through a food mill (using the disc with the smallest holes) into a bowl and then pour into the casserole. Season to taste with salt and pepper and simmer gently for about 10 minutes. To finish, add the beans, mix well, and simmer for 10 more minutes. Makes 4 servings.

Cavolfiore fritto

Fried cauliflower

1 head of cauliflower
4 eggs
Salt
1 cup flour
4 cups vegetable oil
(peanut oil is a good choice)
Lemon wedges, to garnish

Detach the individual flowerets from the cauliflower's main stalk. Leave the smaller flowerets whole and cut the larger ones into pieces about 1 by 2 inches. Discard the main stalk. In a small bowl, beat the eggs with a pinch of salt. Place the cauliflower pieces in a colander, sprinkle the flour over them, and shake well so the flowerets are lightly floured and the excess flour falls through the colander.
Heat the oil in a frying pan to about 375°F. Dip the cauliflower pieces in the egg and deep-fry until golden in the hot oil. Remove the cauliflower from the pan with a strainer-skimmer and drain on paper towels.
Sprinkle with salt and serve hot with lemon wedges.
Makes 4 servings.

Dolci

Latte alla portoghese
Italian custard

5 cups cold milk
Pinch of salt
1 small piece of vanilla bean
1¼ cup granulated sugar
2 large eggs
6 large egg yolks

In a saucepan, heat the milk with the salt, the piece of vanilla bean, and ¼ cup of the sugar. When the mixture reaches the boiling point, simmer slowly over low heat for 30 minutes, using a spoon to skim off the skin that forms on the milk. Remove the saucepan from the heat and allow the milk to cool for 1 hour.

In the meantime, put ¾ cup of the sugar in a small saucepan, preferably of copper, and heat gently until the sugar melts into a brown syrup. Immediately pour the caramelized sugar into a 9-by-5-by-2¾-inch loaf pan and coat the pan evenly by tilting it in all directions. Let cool about 40 minutes.

Preheat oven to 275°F.

In a large bowl, whisk the eggs, egg yolks, and the remaining ¼ cup sugar together until the eggs become lighter in color, then pass the milk through a piece of cheesecloth into the bowl. Blend very well and pour the mixture into the prepared loaf pan.

Place the pan in the preheated oven and bake for 1 to 1¼ hours, or until firm (you can also use a bain-marie, in which case the custard should be left in the oven 15 minutes longer). Remove from the oven and let cool (about 1 hour). Refrigerate for at least 4 hours, then unmold the custard onto a serving dish, cut into slices, and serve. Makes 6 servings.

Zuppa della Cantinetta
Cantinetta biscuit dessert

10 egg yolks
½ cup sugar
2 pounds mascarpone
14 ounces ladyfingers (about 80 wafers)
½ pound semisweet cooking chocolate,
finely chopped
1 bottle *alchermes* (see Glossary)
2 cups espresso (warm)

Whisk egg yolks with the sugar until foamy, then blend in the mascarpone.

Dunk about 20 of the ladyfingers in the *alchermes* and use them to line the bottom of a rectangular baking pan. Spread a layer of the mascarpone cream over these reddish ladyfingers and sprinkle evenly with some of the chopped chocolate. For the next layer, dunk 20 more ladyfingers in the espresso, place them next to each other on the cream, cover with cream, and sprinkle with more chopped chocolate. Repeat to make a total of 4 layers, alternating red and brown, and finish by sprinkling the top with chopped chocolate.

Refrigerate for at least 2 hours to allow it to set.

Makes 20 servings.

Roses growing on the outside walls of houses are a common sight in Tuscany. The best way to discover these kinds of idyllic spots is on extended walks – they are a good place to take a break, and perhaps the owner will even invite you in for a glass of wine or two…

Frittelle di riso
Rice fritters

2 cups milk

½ cup rice (such as Italian Arborio rice; see Glossary)

2 tablespoons butter

1 tablespoon sugar

Pinch of salt

A bit of grated lemon zest

1 tablespoon rum

3 egg yolks

½ cup flour

3 egg whites

Peanut oil, for frying

Cook the rice in the milk, along with the butter, sugar, salt, and lemon zest, until the rice is very soft and has absorbed nearly all the liquid.

Add the rum, egg yolks, and flour, mix well, and allow the mixture to rest overnight, or at least for several hours. Immediately before frying, beat the egg whites until firm and fold carefully into the rice mixture. Use a spoon to make small balls of the mixture and deep-fry them in the peanut oil. Drain well on paper towels and serve hot. Makes 4 servings.

Pan di ramerino

Rosemary bread

1 ounce compressed yeast or 2 packages active dry yeast
Salt
1 cup lukewarm water
5 cups flour
1 sprig of rosemary
Olive oil
¼ cup sugar
⅓ cup raisins
Several coarsely chopped rosemary needles
1 beaten egg, for brushing the bread

Preheat oven to 350°F.

Dissolve the yeast in the lukewarm water with a bit of salt.

Add the flour and knead to make a smooth bread dough.

Let dough rise for about 1 hour. In the meantime, gently sauté the sprig of rosemary in the olive oil for a few minutes, then remove sprig.

When dough has risen, knead well, working in the olive oil from the rosemary sprig, sugar, raisins, and chopped rosemary needles. Shape small, round loaves of bread from the dough and let rise again in a warm place. Then brush with the beaten egg and cut a cross on the top of each ball of dough.

Bake in the preheated oven for about 30 minutes.

Makes 4 servings.

The stone-walled fountains and pools that one finds on the grounds of so many Tuscan estates are fed by groundwater and absolutely essential for the irrigation of the extensive green spaces.

Crostata pasquale di fragole

Easter strawberry tart

For the pastry:
2 cups flour
Pinch of salt
½ cup sugar
6 tablespoons (¾ stick) cold butter
1 egg yolk
3 tablespoons ice water
Dried peas or beans for prebaking crust

For the filling:
1 cup whipping cream
1 tablespoon vanilla sugar (see Glossary)
1 pound fresh strawberries, washed and sliced
Mint leaves, to garnish

Preheat oven to 400°F.

Sift flour together with the salt and sugar. Cut the cold butter into small pieces, add to the flour mixture, and blend together with your fingertips.

Add the egg yolk and ice water, mix together quickly, form the dough into a cake, and refrigerate for about 30 minutes.

Roll out the chilled dough, place in a greased 8-inch spring-form pan, and prebake: line the crust with tinfoil or wax paper, fill with dried peas or beans, and bake for 30 minutes at 400°F. Then remove from the oven, let cool, and take out the peas or beans.

Whip the cream with the vanilla sugar and spread evenly over the bottom of the crust.

Arrange the sliced strawberries in concentric circles on the cream and garnish with fresh mint leaves. Makes 6 servings.

Pesche alla crema di Mascarpone

Summer peaches with mascarpone sauce

3 egg yolks
6 tablespoons sugar
1¼ cups fresh mascarpone cheese
2 tablespoons Cointreau
3 egg whites
4 ripe yellow peaches, peeled and sliced
Sliced, toasted almonds and raspberries,
to garnish

Beat the egg yolks with the sugar until foamy, then carefully blend in the mascarpone and Cointreau.

Whip the egg whites and carefully fold into the egg-mascarpone mixture. Arrange the peach slices in single-serving dessert bowls, pour the mascarpone sauce over them, and chill.

Before serving, garnish with the toasted almonds and raspberries or additional peach wedges. Makes 6 servings.

Summer in Tuscany means fresh fruit. Whether they are used to create an elegant sauce like this one or mixed together in a colorful "macedonia di frutta": the many different fruits available here offer something for every taste.

Crostata di ricotta

Ricotta pie with glacéed fruit

For the crust:

6 tablespoons (¾ stick) sweet butter, cold

1½ cups unbleached all-purpose flour

⅓ cup granulated sugar

1 large egg plus one large egg yolk

For the filling:

2 ounces mixed glacéed fruit

⅓ cup raisins

½ cup white rum

⅓ cup blanched almonds, plus 2 or 3
unblanched almonds

3 large eggs

1 pound ricotta

Grated peel of 1 small lemon

Grated peel of 1 small orange

7 tablespoons granulated sugar

3 tablespoons unbleached all-purpose flour

For the crust: Cut the cold butter into small pieces, mound the flour on a pasta board, make a well in the middle, and put the rest of the crust ingredients into the well. Quickly mix all ingredients in the well together with the flour, shape into a ball, wrap in plastic wrap, and let rest for 30 minutes in the refrigerator.

Meanwhile, make the filling: Chop the glacéed fruit, mix with the raisins and the rum in a small bowl, and let soak 20 to 25 minutes. In the meantime, grind all the almonds very fine in a food processor.

Separate one of the eggs, add the egg white to the almonds (saving the egg yolk), and mix well.

Drain the ricotta in a piece of cheesecloth, place in a large bowl, and mix very well with the 2 remaining eggs and the egg yolk. Add the orange and lemon peel to the ricotta mixture, drain the glacéed fruit and raisins (discarding the rum), and add the fruit mixture, along with the almond/egg-white mixture and the sugar, to the ricotta. Blend thoroughly, mix in the flour, and set aside.

Butter a 9-inch springform pan and preheat the oven to 375°F. With a rolling pin, roll the dough out until about ⅜ inch thick (this can also be done between two sheets of plastic wrap to prevent the dough from breaking) and line the springform pan with it, letting the excess hang over the sides.

Spread the filling evenly over the dough. Trim off excess dough, form into ½-inch strips, and place strips in a crisscross pattern on top.

Bake in the preheated oven about 40 minutes. Allow the *crostata* to cool about 30 minutes before removing it from the pan. Serve warm or cold. Makes 6 servings.

WINE RECOMMENDATION: *Muffato della Sala Umbria IGT*

Ciambellone

Italian ring cake

Raisins as desired
⅓ cup liqueur
3 eggs
1⅓ cups sugar
½ cup milk
5 cups flour
1 tablespoon baking powder
5 tablespoons butter, softened
Bread crumbs

Preheat oven to 350°F. Soak the raisins in the liqueur.
In a large bowl, whisk the eggs together with the sugar, then gradually mix in the milk. Sift the flour together with the baking powder and stir into the mixture, along with the butter, liqueur, and raisins.
Grease a tube pan (or a normal round baking pan with a cup placed in the middle) with oil or butter and dust with bread crumbs to prevent the batter from sticking. Pour the batter into the pan and bake immediately in the preheated oven 40 to 45 minutes. Do not overbake or bake too hot. To test for doneness, insert a toothpick in the center: if it comes out clean, the cake is done. Makes one cake.

Schiacciata con l'uva

Sweet focaccia with red grapes

1 ounce compressed yeast or 2 packages active dry yeast
¾ cup warm water
3¼ cups flour
Pinch of salt
¾ cup olive oil
1 tablespoon rosemary needles
½ cup sugar
1 pound red grapes

Preheat oven to 425°F.

Dissolve the yeast in the warm water, mix in the flour and salt, and knead until smooth and elastic.

Let rise at room temperature until doubled in size.

In a small saucepan, heat the rosemary needles in the olive oil, strain the oil, and let cool.

Mix the oil (which now has a rosemary flavor) and ¼ cup of the sugar into the risen dough. Spread the dough into a 10-by-2-inch baking dish, arrange the grapes over the top, sprinkle with the remaining sugar, and bake in the preheated oven about 20 minutes. Makes 6 servings.

WINE RECOMMENDATION: *Aleatico Maremma Toscana IGT*

For centuries, wine has been the national beverage and virtually the national occupation in Italy. Tuscany – which next to Piedmont is Italy's most famous winegrowing region – has alone over 150,000 acres of vineyards. But grapes do not always have to be pressed; they can also be used whole to create a variety of delicious desserts.

Torta di mele della fattoressa
Farm apple cake

5 cooking apples

3 eggs

6 tablespoons sugar

4 tablespoons (½ stick) soft butter

½ teaspoon cinnamon

½ teaspoon grated lemon zest

6 tablespoons flour

1 teaspoon baking powder

1 teaspoon vanilla sugar (see Glossary)

2 tablespoons Vin Santo

Preheat oven to 350°F.

Peel, core, and quarter the apples, then cut the quarters into thin slices.

Beat the eggs with the sugar until foamy. Add the butter, cinnamon, and lemon zest to the beaten eggs.

Sift together the flour, baking powder, and vanilla sugar, and mix gently into the batter along with the Vin Santo. Stir in the sliced apples, pour batter into a greased springform pan, and bake in the preheated oven about 40 minutes. Makes 6 servings.

WINE RECOMMENDATION: *Muffato della Sala Umbria IGT*

Castagnaccio

Chestnut cake

4 cups chestnut flour
2 to 3 cups cold water
Pinch of salt
Rosemary needles (optional)
1 tablespoon olive oil
¼ cup raisins
⅓ cup pine nuts
⅓ cup coarsely chopped walnuts

Preheat oven to 350°F.

Sift the chestnut flour to avoid lumps, place in a large bowl with the cold water, salt, and several rosemary needles, if desired, and mix to make a rather thin batter. The olive oil can be stirred in at this point or used later to drizzle over the batter in the pan.

Grease a wide baking pan and pour in the batter. The batter should be about ½ inch deep in the pan, but if you prefer a crunchier cake, use a bit less chestnut flour to make the batter shallower. Sprinkle with raisins, pine nuts, and walnuts, and bake in the preheated oven 30 to 40 minutes. The *castagnaccio* is done when it begins to give off a lovely aroma, takes on a dark-brown color, and small cracks start to develop on the surface. Makes 1 cake.

WINE RECOMMENDATION: *Vin Santo del Chianti Classico DOC Tenute Marchese Antinori*

The Antinori family has been making wine for over 600 years. Experience and the courage to experiment have made this family-run business one of Europe's leading producers of quality wines.

Bruciate briache
"Drunken" chestnuts

16 sweet chestnuts
⅓ cup grappa
Sugar

Using a sharp paring knife, make slits in the peel of each chestnut. If the chestnuts are to be roasted over an open fire, place them in a long-handled, perforated pan and shake them occasionally while they cook (10 to 15 minutes). The chestnuts can also be cooked in a preheated oven at 170°F for 15 to 20 minutes. When the chestnuts are done inside and the outer shell is slightly charred, remove from the fire or oven and let cool about 10 minutes.

Peel the chestnuts, place in a small stockpot, and douse with the grappa. Flambé, sprinkle with a bit of sugar, and serve. Makes 4 servings.

WINE RECOMMENDATION: *San Giocondo Vino Novello Toscana IGT*

Ballotte
Boiled chestnuts

16 sweet chestnuts
Water
Salt
10 seeds from wild fennel
1 bay leaf

Boil the chestnuts in a large pot with water, plenty of salt, fennel seeds, and/or bay leaf (depending on your taste). If fresh chestnuts are used, they should be cooked through in about 30 minutes. Place the pot on the table, take out the chestnuts one at a time, peel while still hot, and enjoy. Makes 4 servings.

Schiacciata alla fiorentina

Florentine sponge cake

4 cups flour
1 tablespoon baking powder
¾ cup sugar
1 egg
Grated peel of one orange
Juice of one orange
¼ cup olive oil
½ cup milk
Vanilla sugar (see Glossary)

Preheat oven to 350°F.
Sift the flour together with the baking powder. Beat the sugar and egg until foamy, stir in the orange peel and juice, then add the oil and milk. Gradually blend in the flour mixture and pour batter into a buttered jellyroll pan. Bake in the preheated oven until golden brown, about 20 minutes. Remove from oven, let cool, and sprinkle with a bit of vanilla sugar.
Makes one cake.

WINE RECOMMENDATION: *Aleatico Maremma Toscana IGT*

Tuscany is well worth a trip any season of the year. If you visit this region in winter, you will be rewarded with culinary delicacies that are served only when outside the cold wind sweeps around the mighty stone houses and inside an open fire crackles in the hearth. Even desserts are seasonal: this orange-flavored cake, for example, is typically served during the colder months.

Cantucci col Vin santo

Almond cookies with Vin Santo

2 cups flour
½ teaspoon baking powder
⅔ cup sugar
Pinch of salt
3 large eggs
1 teaspoon vanilla
1 cup peeled almonds

Preheat oven to 350°F.

Mix the flour with the baking powder, sugar, and salt. Make a well, and in its center beat together the eggs and vanilla, gradually drawing in the dry ingredients to make a soft dough. Let rest for 5 minutes, then work in the almonds.

Shape the dough into 2 logs, place in a buttered baking pan, and bake until golden brown, about 30 minutes. Cut vertically into ½-inch slices and return to the oven to bake another 10 to 15 minutes. Makes 6 servings.

Cenci

Tuscan dough bows

2½ cups flour
2 tablespoons butter
¼ cup sugar
2 eggs
1 tablespoon rum or Vin Santo
Pinch of salt
1 tablespoon grated orange peel (optional)
1 teaspoon baking powder (optional)

Vanilla sugar, to garnish (see Glossary)
Peanut oil, for frying

Work all ingredients together to make a firm dough – to turn out well it really needs to be thoroughly kneaded by hand (if you prefer your *cenci* a bit softer, add 1 teaspoon baking powder to the mixture). Wrap dough in a kitchen towel and let rest at least 1 hour.

If the dough is too sticky, add a bit more flour.

Roll out the dough very thin and use a knife or pastry-cutting wheel to cut it into 1-by-8-inch strips. Gently twist these strips and tie them in bows, or use your imagination to shape them in other ways. Deep-fry in the peanut oil, drain well on paper towels, let cool, and sprinkle with vanilla sugar.

Serve the *cenci* (the Italian word for rags) in a dessert bowl.
Makes 1 large bowl of *cenci*.

Glossary

ALCHERMES: a typically Italian spicy liqueur, reddish in color

AL DENTE: "to the teeth" – designates the correct degree of doneness when cooking pasta or vegetables; the food should be firm but not hard

ALL'ONDA: refers to the soft, slightly fluid texture of the perfect risotto; if you tilt the plate, the risotto ripples in waves – *all'onda*

ALL'UOVO: refers to a pasta made with eggs

ARBORIO RICE: a round-grained rice grown primarily in the Po Valley; used in particular for risotto

BAIN-MARIE: French term for a technique by which a pan or bowl of food is placed in a large, shallow pan of warm water, which surrounds the food with gentle, even heat

BONE: to remove the bones from meat, fish or fowl (but the muscle cords should remain intact, if possible, so use a sharp knife with a very thin blade to cut along the natural seams of the meat)

BORLOTTI BEANS: also known as cranberry beans; a reddish-brown, speckled bean variety with a slightly bittersweet flavor, ideal for soups and casseroles

BRUSCHETTA: slices of toasted bread rubbed with garlic, drizzled with olive oil, and covered with a variety of toppings

CANNELLINI BEANS: a small, white, kidney-shaped bean well suited for salads and casseroles

CASTELLUCCIO LENTILS: a small, brown mountain lentil variety cultivated near Castelluccio, Umbria, at an elevation of about 4,500 feet; has a particularly nutty savor, requires no presoaking, and is ideal for cold dishes

CAVOLO NERO: known in English as black leaf kale or Tuscan cabbage; a dark-green leafy vegetable sold as loose leaves (not in heads)

CIPOLLA ROSSA DI TROPEA: a slightly sweet variety of red onion named after the southern Italian city of Tropea

CONCHIGLIE: a type of Italian pasta shaped like a seashell

CROSTINI: "little toasts," small slices of grilled or toasted bread that can have a variety of toppings, such as cheese, ham, or vegetables, or simply brushed with olive oil; see also Bruschetta

EMMER: also known as farro; a variety of wheat that was a staple grain as far back as early Roman times

FETTUCCINE: narrow Italian ribbon pasta

SEMOLINA: flour made from durum wheat, available in many supermarkets

CHESTNUT FLOUR: ground sweet chestnuts, available in many natural-foods stores

CHICKPEA FLOUR: made from ground chickpeas (garbanzo beans); available in natural-foods stores

LUMACONI: snail-shaped Italian pasta

MEZZE MANICHE (rigate): a wide tube of pasta that is a shorter version of rigatoni

PECORINO FRESCO: young pecorino with a mild, slightly sour flavor; when very fresh it is white and has a crumbly texture

PECORINO: Italian cheese made from ewe's milk

PEPERONCINO, PEPERONCINI: Italian term for chili peppers, which exist in a variety of forms and degrees of hotness; can be used fresh or as dried pepper flakes

POLENTA: a mush made from cornmeal

PROSCIUTTO: raw ham from Italy

RISOTTO RICE: a round-grained rice grown primarily in Italy's Po Valley; see also Arborio

SALAME TOSCANO: a very aromatic, strongly seasoned salami from Tuscany

SALSICCIA DOLCI: mild Italian sausage

SALSICCIA: spicier Italian sausage

SCAMORZA: a pear-shaped Italian cheese; its unique shape comes from being hung from the ceiling during the ripening process.

SPAGHETTINI: a thin type of spaghetti

STRACCHINO: a type of cow's-milk cheese typical of Lombardy

TOMATOES, PEELED: blanching the tomatoes first makes the skin easier to remove (alternately, use peeled tomatoes out of the can)

TORTELLI: a stuffed pasta made in a variety of shapes

VANILLA SUGAR: a vanilla-flavored sugar frequently used in Tuscan desserts; it is not readily available outside Europe but can easily be prepared at home by placing 1 or 2 vanilla pods in an airtight container with 2 cups granulated sugar and then waiting a week for the sugar to become infused with the flavor of the vanilla

WILD FENNEL: contains more essential oil than the cultivated type, but if the former is not available, the latter is an acceptable substitute

Index of recipes

Conversions of weights and measures

Fluid volume

1 teaspoon = 5 ml
1 tablespoon (3 teaspoons) = 15 ml
¼ cup (4 tablespoons) = 60 ml
⅓ cup = 80 ml
½ cup = 120 ml
⅔ cup = 160 ml
¾ cup = 180 ml
1 cup = 240 ml
1 quart = 946 ml

In cases where great precision is not necessary, these conversions can be rounded off as follows:
1 cup = 250 ml
1 quart = 1 liter

Weight

1 ounce = 28 g
4 ounces (¼ pound) = 113 g
8 ounces (½ pound) = 230 g
12 ounces (¾ pound) = 340 g
1 pound (16 ounces) = 450 g

Weights of common ingredients in grams

Flour, all purpose or chickpea: 1 cup = 120 g
Sugar: 1 cup = 200 g
Rice, uncooked: 1 cup = 190 g
Butter: 1 tablespoon = 15 g
Parmesan cheese, grated: 1 cup = 90 g

Linear measures

⅛ inch = 3 mm
¼ inch = 6 mm
½ inch = 13 mm
1 inch = 2.5 cm

Approximate temperature conversions

To convert Fahrenheit into Centigrade (Celsius), subtract 32, multiply by 5, then divide by 9.

275°F = 140°C = Gas Mark 1
300°F = 150°C = Gas Mark 2
325°F = 170°C = Gas Mark 3
350°F = 180°C = Gas Mark 4
375°F = 190°C = Gas Mark 5
400°F = 200°C = Gas Mark 6
425°F = 220°C = Gas Mark 7
450°F = 230°C = Gas Mark 8
475°F = 240°C = Gas Mark 9

Addresses

Cantinetta Antinori in Florence

The first Cantinetta opened its doors in 1957 –
in Palazzo Antinori, one of the loveliest examples
of Florentine architecture of the mid-fifteenth
century.

Piazza Antinori 3
50123 – Florence
+39 (0) 55 292 234
firenze@cantinetta-antinori.com

Cantinetta Antinori in Zürich

In 1994 the first Cantinetta outside Italy opened:
in Zürich, Switzerland.
This idea came from Piero Antinori and Rudi
Bindella, owner of the wine and food company
of the same name, which has been distributing
Antinori wines in Switzerland since 1955.
The restaurant is located in the historic center
of the city, just off the famous Bahnhofstrasse and
near Lake Zürich.

Augustinergasse 25
8001 Zürich
+41 (0) 44 211 72 10
zurigo@cantinetta-antinori.com

Cantinetta Antinori in Vienna

Following the great success of the Cantinetta in
Zürich, a Cantinetta Antinori was opened in
Vienna in 1995, located in a historic building in
the center of town, in view of the city's most famous landmark, Saint Stephan's Cathedral.
The restaurant's interior walls are painted with
frescoes of lovely Italian paintings and decorated
with marble statues and mirrors from the
Renaissance.

Jasomirgottstrasse 3–5
1010 Vienna
+43 (0) 1 533 77 22
vienna@cantinetta-antinori.com

Cantinetta Antinori in Moscow

In 2004 the Antinoris ventured into Russia,
opening a Cantinetta Antinori in Moscow, which
quickly became one of the most famous restaurants in the Russian capital. It is situated in the
very heart of the city, in a historic nineteenth-
century mansion.

20 Denezhny Pereulok
Moscow
+7 (499) 241 37 71
mosca@cantinetta-antinori.com